Growing Your
Library Career
with Social Media

Chandos Advances in Information Series

Growing Your Library Career with Social Media

DANIELLA SMITH
Associate Professor, Department of Information Science
College of Information, University of North Texas,
United States

CP
CHANDOS
PUBLISHING
An imprint of Elsevier

Chandos Publishing is an imprint of Elsevier
50 Hampshire Street, 5th Floor, Cambridge, MA 02139, United States
The Boulevard, Langford Lane, Kidlington, OX5 1GB, United Kingdom

Notices
Knowledge and best practice in this field are constantly changing. As new research and experience
broaden our understanding, changes in research methods, professional practices, or medical
treatment may become necessary.

Practitioners and researchers must always rely on their own experience and knowledge in
evaluating and using any information, methods, compounds, or experiments described herein. In
using such information or methods they should be mindful of their own safety and the safety of
others, including parties for whom they have a professional responsibility.

To the fullest extent of the law, neither the Publisher nor the authors, contributors, or editors,
assume any liability for any injury and/or damage to persons or property as a matter of products
liability, negligence or otherwise, or from any use or operation of any methods, products,
instructions, or ideas contained in the material herein.

British Library Cataloguing-in-Publication Data
A catalogue record for this book is available from the British Library

Library of Congress Cataloging-in-Publication Data
A catalog record for this book is available from the Library of Congress

ISBN: 978-0-08-102411-9 (print)

ISBN: 978-0-08-102412-6 (online)

For information on all Chandos Publishing publications
visit our website at https://www.elsevier.com/books-and-journals

  **Working together
to grow libraries in
developing countries**

www.elsevier.com • www.bookaid.org

Publisher: Glyn Jones
Acquisition Editor: Glyn Jones
Editorial Project Manager: Mariana L. Khul
Production Project Manager: Debasish Ghosh
Cover Designer: Matthew Limbert

Typeset by MPS Limited, Chennai, India

CONTENTS

BIOGRAPHY

Dr. Smith is an Associate Professor in the Department of Information Science at the University of North Texas. She is a member of several state, national, and international organizations, including the American Library Association and the American Association of School Librarians. She currently serves as an ALA Councilor At-Large and is a blogger for AASL (http://knowledgequest.aasl.org/author/dsmith/). Dr. Smith has worked in various facets of librarianship and education, including being a research program coordinator in a university center, a classroom teacher, a youth services public librarian, and a school librarian. Her research interests include the leadership behaviors of librarians, youth information seeking behaviors, technology implementation in schools, and the use of social media for information seeking.

ACKNOWLEDGMENTS

Completing this book was nothing less than a journey. It is dedicated to my mother, my husband, and my children. I am grateful to my mother for being courageous and reminding me that limitations exist when I allow them to be in place. She will always be in my heart. I am thankful to my husband for being my biggest advocate and to my children for being proud of their mother.

I am much obliged to my assistants for searching dutifully for the materials that I requested. I appreciate the time that Dr. Jason Alston, Dr. Spencer Keralis, Kelly Hoppe, kYmberly Keeton, and Ayla Stein took to share their knowledge. Thank you to Elsevier's Mariana Kühl Leme and Debasish Ghosh for their patience and guidance throughout the process. I am appreciative of Dr. George Knott for believing that I could complete this project.

I praise God for blessing me with the words to finish.

Sincerely,
Daniella L. Smith

CHAPTER 1

Social Media in Society

Figure 1.1 Social media scribble.

1.1 DEFINING SOCIAL MEDIA

Tim Berners-Lee introduced the World Wide Web (WWW) in August 1991 and changed the world forever. When discussing the intention that underpinned his creation, Berners-Lee noted, "The original thing I wanted to do was make it a collaborative medium, a place where we can all meet and read and write …. Collaborative things are exciting, and the fact people are doing wikis and blogs shows they're (embracing) its creative side" (as cited by Carver, 2005, para. 3). While Berners-Lee may have envisioned a creative force, his creation has continued to evolve to become increasingly interactive and participatory each year. Initially, the WWW required input from a webmaster who would control the information via a platform such as a website. The early version of the WWW allowed very little interaction between website creators and users (Scott & Orlikowski, 2012). Today, it has become easier to share content, and webmasters and a world of Internet surfers can now create their own content to add to the Internet.

Growing Your Library Career with Social Media
DOI: https://doi.org/10.1016/B978-0-08-102411-9.00001-7

The Internet has also enabled people to form online social networks. Mathews (2007) noted that the term social networking is not new. In fact, it was first mentioned by J.A. Barnes in 1954. Mathews further asserted that social networking has been studied by a variety of researchers in fields that include anthropology, psychology, organizational studies, and information science—the field that is highly relevant to librarians. Social networking theory is based on the idea that relationships are connected nodes. Each of these nodes can be analyzed according to the strength of their association with one another. In this way, social networking helps individuals to build social capital through which they can improve the quality of their lives.

According to Sloan and Quan-Hasse (2017), social media, which thrives on online social networking has grown considerably since 2007, and the growth has had economic, social, and political ramifications. Sloan and Quan-Hasse also note that the definition of social media is highly disputed. As such, it is often defined according to the platforms on which it is published as opposed to being based on a concrete definition. Since platforms for social media are diverse and continually evolving, for the purposes of this book, social media includes, but is not limited to, blogs, microblogs, social networking sites, wikis, audio sharing sites, video sharing sites, picture sharing sites, forums, and social news sites. After examining 23 definitions and 179 articles about social media, Ouirdi, El Ouirdi, Sergers, and Henderickx (2014, p. 123) offered the following comprehensive definition to account for ongoing changes in social media platforms:

A set of mobile and web-based platforms built on Web 2.0 technologies, and allowing users at the micro-, meso- and macro-levels to share and geo-tag user-generated content (images, text, audio, video, and games), to collaborate, and to build networks and communities, with the possibility of reaching and involving large audiences. (p. 123)

boyd and Ellison (2007) describe the history of social media and state:

We define social network sites as web-based services that allow individuals to (1) construct a public or semi-public profile within a bounded system, (2) articulate a list of other users with whom - they share a connection, and (3) view and traverse their list of connections and those made by others within the system. The nature and nomenclature of these connections may vary from site to site. (p. 211)

Citing Haythornthwaite's (2005) theory of latent ties, boyd and Ellison go on to differentiate between sharing information on a social media site with existing users and the desire to network and meet new people. In some cases, social network site users may just want to interact with people on a certain social networking site or use the website to organize their information.

Profiles are a prominent feature of many social networking sites that help users determine who they would like to interact with. According to boyd and Ellison (2007), these profiles allow site users to create pages that display their unique characteristics. These profiles are generated by completing the forms that are available on the social networking sites and may include the ability to add pictures, videos, and answer questions that identify user details such as the location, interests, and age. Social media sites often let users manipulate the privacy settings associated with these profiles so that they can make them private or visible to search engines.

As users display their profiles, they may use them to develop a network of "friends". The term that is used to describe these social contacts varies according to the network; for example, they may be referred to as contacts or followers. boyd (2006) indicates that a "friend" on a social media site may differ from the concept of a friend in the physical face-to-face world. This is because "friends" on social media may be individuals who a person never meets or physically interacts with. However, regardless of the true personal connection, being able to publicly display the number of "friends" that one has on social media is a feature social media site users enjoy because it is a sign of popularity.

The ability to leave comments and send public and private messages is an important part of some social networking websites and, again, this functionality can differ according to the site itself. The availability of the features may also be limited according to the pricing plans that are available for a social network. For example, LinkedIn does not allow private messaging unless a member pays for the premium plan. In addition, the premium plan for LinkedIn allows users to see everyone who has reviewed their profile in the last 90 days and view analytics about how their information is being accessed.

Social media sites are unique in the features that they may offer participants. For example, Snapchat (www.snapchat.com) is a social networking site that utilizes a messaging app for sharing videos and pictures. Users send videos and pictures using a mobile app. Although creators of pictures and videos may save them before sending them, after a person views them, the pictures or videos may self-destruct within seconds.

Alternatively, Snapchat users may start a video call or create a 24-hour collection of videos and pictures (i.e., snaps).

Twitter (www.twitter.com) is a microblogging social media and news site through which users can send messages that contain up to 140 characters. According to Rosen (2017), in September 2017, Twitter was considering allowing longer Tweets of up to 280 characters and was prototyping the idea with a small group of users. While people who are not registered can read messages, one must be a registered user to send them. Users may attach pictures and include links that reference materials such as videos, articles, and longer social media posts. Readers can review trending topics and include identifiers called hashtags to indicate the topic of posts. While some content is recreational, business and individuals alike use Twitter to share information. When registered users deem information they access online to be of importance, they can retweet it, like it, and save it to a moment.

Statista (2018) notes that the lines between virtual and face-to-face lives continue to blur. The most popular social networks are typically available in multiple languages and can connect people regardless of geographic, political, and economic circumstances. Most adults (88%) in the United States use the Internet for some reason (Pew Research Center, 2016). The same report specified that 68% of adults without a high school diploma, 81% with a high school diploma, 94% with some college-level education, and 98% of adults with full college-level education use the Internet, making it important for people of all backgrounds, regardless of their education level. According to Statista (2018), social media networks have different focuses. For example, Facebook and Google + focus on connecting users with friends and family and use social games to enhance their experiences. Twitter and Tumblr are microblogging platforms that specialize in the rapid release of information (Box 1.1).

BOX 1.1 How did you get started with social media?

Ayla Stein—My involvement began with a requirement for class. I had a literacy class or active learning class, and we talked about different kinds of social media tools. Then I met a bunch of librarians. I was very interested in digital humanities, but I didn't really know how to reach out to people. So, I just followed a bunch of digital humanities people in hashtags, and that's how I started building my professional network.

1.2 WORK

Increasing numbers of employers are engaging in the controversial practice of screening current and potential employees by examining their online presence. This trend has developed in tandem with the popularity of social networks such as Facebook, LinkedIn, and Twitter, as well as blogs and online alumni associations (Jeske & Shultz, 2016).

Meanwhile, the boundaries between what is considered personal and professional have continued to blur. Even when posting personal information online with strict privacy settings activated, controlling one's digital footprint is difficult, since anyone can share this information within personal networks or it can be hacked by an outsider for malicious purposes. Hence, it is important to monitor personal branding and how one is presented online at all times.

In addition to screening employees through social media, organizations are adopting social media guidelines or policies. Jeske and Shultz (2016) state that these policies are important for two reasons. First, they help improve job security by educating employees about expectations—in other words, employees are less likely to be fired due to inappropriate online behavior when the parameters of usage are clearly indicated. Second, in addition to being used to screen for undesirable candidates, social media can be used to attract suitable ones. Consequently, as Lam (2015) notes, social media places employers in a precarious position. While using it to screen employees and applicants can be seen as an invasion of privacy, failing to do so could lead to suboptimal staffing outcomes.

An example of an employer screening an employee's online activity was demonstrated by ESPN in September 2017 (Stelter, 2017). Jemele Hill, a popular host for the network, used her Twitter account to assert that President Donald Trump was a white supremacist, had succeeded through his connections to white supremacy, and was "ignorant" and "offensive." Sara Huckabee Sanders, the White House Press Secretary, responded by calling for Hill to be fired for her Tweets. Under scrutiny from her employers, Hill issued a statement emphasizing that her comments reflected her personal beliefs, not the network's perspective. She went on to say, "My regret is that my comments and the public way I made them painted ESPN in an unfair light. My respect for the company and my colleagues remains unconditional" (as cited by Stelter, 2017, para. 7). ESPN then issued its own statement: "Jemele has a right to her personal opinions, but not to publicly share them on a platform that implies that she was in any way speaking on behalf of ESPN. She has acknowledged that her Tweets crossed that line and has apologized for doing so. We accept her apology" (as cited by Stelter, 2017, para. 7). While Hill remained on the air after the incident, her experience is an example of how employers can monitor employees on social media and make hiring and firing decisions based on their activity. ESPN clearly found Hill's personal comments, publicly made, to be detrimental to its image; potentially, they could have resulted in irreparable damage to Hill's career.

Another example of how social media interactions can impact an individual's professional status can be observed in a case that took place in September 2017 when Cammie Rone, a second-grade teacher from Mississippi's South Panola School District, posted on her Facebook page: "If blacks in this country are so offended no one is forcing them to stay here. Why don't they pack up and move back to Africa where they will have to work for a living? I am sure our government will pay for it! We pay for everything else" (as cited by Fowler, 2017, para. 4). Rone claimed that her Facebook page had been hacked but, ultimately, following an investigation, she was fired by the school district.

1.3 POLITICS

Social media increasingly permeates political discourse, as the story of Jemele Hill shows. Joy Reid, an MSNBC host, reacted to Hill's predicament by stating during her TV show, "Today, the White House press secretary used the people's podium to call for the firing of an individual citizen, @jemelehill. Take that in" (as cited by Stelter, 2017, para. 22).

As discourse from social media is discussed on the news, social media has been successfully used to organize political protests and build political communities. It is frequently used by whistle-blowers—WikiLeaks, for example—which attracts the attention of media outlets (Aslam, 2016). Aslam (2016) further notes that social media has crossover appeal. News that is overlooked by traditional media outlets is instantly delivered to the masses. Social networks often disseminate trending topics before they can be addressed on the news. Other examples include the Egyptian revolution and Occupy Wall Street, both of which began in 2011 (Fuchs, 2017). In these instances, protesters used networks, such as Facebook and Twitter, in conjunction with their mobile phones to organize their communities.

Freedom House (https://freedomhouse.org) is an independent watchdog organization that was established in 1941 to promote democracy around the world. One of its most recent projects involved an examination of the effect that social media has on politics. The resulting report, "Freedom on the Net 2017: Manipulating Social Media to Undermine Democracy," concludes that while Internet usage in the United States is relatively open, online political discourse is characterized by "a proliferation of fabricated news articles, divisive partisan vitriol, and aggressive harassment of many journalists" (Freedom House, 2017, p. 2).

After the 2017 US presidential election, claims were made that Russia interfered with the election by posting propaganda and fake news online to manipulate the perspectives of unsuspecting voters. As investigations were launched into the alleged interference, evidence that social media had been used to manipulate political outcomes in other countries started to surface. Freedom House's report suggests that misinformation introduced on social media has influenced elections in no less than 18 countries by impairing citizens' ability to make informed, fact-based decisions.

The dissemination of propaganda is by no means confined to foreign meddling. Freedom House (2017) notes that of the 3.4 billion people worldwide who have access to the Internet, 42% live "in countries where the government employs armies of 'opinion shapers' to spread government views and counter critics on social media" (p. 7). Political opponents seeking to win elections or sway public opinion likewise often seek opportunities to manipulate social media content. After surveying 65 countries as part of its research, Freedom House found that social media manipulation tactics include paid pro-government commentators, pro-government media and propaganda, fake news about elections, and hijacked social media accounts. While information from paid pro-government commentators stems from credible reports, the commentators often do not disclose that they are posting information on behalf of the government. Fake news, on the other hand, merely mimics credible reports and is false. Pro-government media and propaganda may be orchestrated by the government or affiliated individuals/organizations. A government may bribe online commentators, take over their social media accounts, and distribute political editorials through their profiles.

1.4 EDUCATION

Social media has also become an issue in the educational system. Warnick, Bitters, Falk, and Kim (2016) see teachers as moral pillars of the community who should exhibit ethical behavior both during and outside working hours. They recommend that teachers be held accountable for their actions—whether unprofessional, inappropriate, or illegal—on social media. Problematic behaviors from teachers include writing comments that disparage the school community, publishing racial slurs, or contacting students personally. Warnick et al. (2016) identify four overlapping categories where problems arise for teachers on social media:

- Statements placed on social media that reflect poor professional judgment.
- Posts on social media that reveal that teachers have engaged in reckless or illegal behavior.
- Comments, posts, and pictures that make students uncomfortable and bring unwanted attention to them.
- Behaviors displayed on social media that contradict norms within their communities. (p. 776)

While it is recommended that teachers should be punished for unbecoming online behavior, there is no suggestion that teachers should be prevented from using social media. Indeed, Warnick et al. (2016) acknowledge that social media is useful for educational purposes. Prohibiting educators from using social media for teaching can potentially limit the resources that students have available.

1.5 CHILD DEVELOPMENT AND FAMILY DYNAMICS

Twenge (2017) makes several observations about how society has changed with the advent of social media and how social media has forged differences across familial generations. She argues that a shift in social behavior became evident between 2007 and 2009, when the rate of smartphone ownership in the United States first exceeded 50% of the population. Smartphones make it particularly easy to access social networks; in fact, research by the Pew Research Center (2009) indicates that impoverished students without access to computers at home still use their smartphones to access the Internet.

Twenge (2017) refers to the generation born between 1995 and 2012 - as the iGen. This generation differs from their parents in that they have never known a time when the widespread use of the Internet did not exist (they also were/are likely to use social media before they started/start high school). She observes how many contemporary children spend more time in the presence of, yet not emotionally connecting with, their families. Though they are in close physical proximity, they are

BOX 1.2 How do you keep social media from being a distraction?

kYmberly Keeton—I do not post on the weekends. Social media is a part of what I do. So, when I am online using these platforms, I do what I need to do and log off. I typically check for responses late at night. I respond to inquiries the following day.

Ayla Stein—I try not to have it on my browser unless I'm doing a specific Twitter chat, or I want to ask a specific person a question, like during work. And if I do get on it, I use my phone during breaks.

A lot of people will have notifications on their phone. I don't like to hear a chime every other minute. I have the notifications turned off. I also do not have browser notifications. I would never be able to concentrate.

distracted by social media on devices such as tablets and smartphones. Furthermore, because children are spending more time interacting in cyberspace, their activities are less likely to be monitored than those of generations past. Parents are unlikely to sit next to their children and watch everything that is happening on their screens. To make matters more complicated, some social media websites—such as Snapchat, which allows users to send videos that disappear within seconds of being watched—make it particularly easy for children to avoid parental monitoring (Box 1.2).

1.6 THE LEGAL IMPLICATIONS OF SOCIAL MEDIA

After keeping it a secret for 20 years, Amy Hestir, a woman from Columbia, Missouri, finally broke her silence about a teacher who allegedly sexually abused her while she was a 12-year-old student in junior high (Martin, 2011). Upon learning that her rapist was still working in the school system, Hestir reported him, but no action was taken. She later contacted Jane Cunningham, a Missouri senator at the time, who began working on a student protection bill that was eventually passed, in 2011, in the form of the Amy Hestir Student Protection Act (Martin, 2011).

The Act was designed to protect students from sexually inappropriate or predatory teachers, and part of it required school districts to create social media communication policies to provide guidelines for interactions between students and teachers. In response, the Missouri State Teachers Association created a model social media policy for school districts. While the policy acknowledged that electronic communication for work purposes is now the norm, it called for this communication to be monitored. It did not propose prohibiting employees from using electronic communication for non-work purposes but warned that such communication should be regulated by local, state, and federal law.

Section 162.069 of the Act, however, went further, prohibiting teachers from creating or using "a non-work-related Internet site which allows exclusive access with a current or former student." Soon after the Act was passed, Section 162.069 was repealed by Missouri's then governor, Jay Nixon, who argued that it was much too restrictive in terms of teachers' free speech. By repealing Section 162.069, Nixon provided teachers with the freedom to potentially utilize Internet sites to interact with students online. However, school districts were still required to develop social media policies.

Noting Section 162.069 of the Amy Hestir Act, Baez and Caulfield (2012) argue that restrictive social media policies may discourage qualified teaching candidates from applying for positions because they want to preserve their privacy. If this becomes the case, schools will find the pool of qualified candidates that they have access to relatively limited. Baez and Caulfield cite the example of a teacher's aide, Kimberly Hester, who was fired from her job for refusing to provide her employers with her social media username and password. Rather than risk having to give up their online privacy, many educators will seek out jobs with less intrusive employers. This supports Governor Nixon's assertion that closely monitoring the social media presence of teachers can be interpreted as a violation of their First Amendment rights.

Although the state of Missouri legislature has acted to protect students in its school districts, many other state legislatures have not. Even so, policies have been developed by school districts throughout the country. For example, the Massachusetts Association of School Committees created a social media policy as a statewide example. The policy encourages superintendents to act against inappropriate activities such as becoming friends and/or exchanging contact details with students on social media and warns employees that such actions will result in punitive action. Similarly, in response to a teacher's derogatory online statements about students, a Pennsylvania school district created a policy that "banned online activities by teachers that would jeopardize the professional nature of the staff-student relationship" (Baez & Caulfield, 2012, p. 274).

The legal implications of social media are vast. Outside of relationships with employees, many companies find themselves in trouble with social media. For example, for many companies, posting to platforms such as Facebook increases the popularity of their products and positively impacts sales. Mentioning a celebrity in connection with a product will significantly increase a given post's reach; however, obtaining the celebrity's permission to do so is extremely important. Many companies have found themselves encountering lawsuits from celebrities after posting pictures of these celebrities using their products without first obtaining formal consent (Cook, 2016).

1.7 CONCLUSION

While this section is not intended to discourage the use of social media, it is designed to provide an overview of its impact, which is not always positive. Social media has many implications for the fabric of society—from our homes, to our workplaces, to our schools, it has embedded itself in the ways in which we think and act. Whatever benefits social media brings should be weighed carefully against its associated costs and difficulties; how we actually use social media should be open to question. Social media may seem like an ephemeral diversion; however, it can have a lasting effect on our lives.

1.8 CHAPTER CHALLENGES

1. Look at the social media policies of your university or job. What restrictions are present? Are you following them?
2. Interview a librarian at your school or job and ask them the steps that they take to adhere to the social media policies that are in place.

REFERENCES

Aslam, R. (2016). Building peace through journalism in the social/alternate media. *Media and Communications*, *4*(1), 63−79. Retrieved from ⟨http://www.cogitatiopress.com/mediaandcommunication/article/view/371/371⟩ (accessed 17.09.15).

Baez, J., & Caulfield, K. (2012). Drawing line in the shifting sand of social media: Attempting to prevent teachers from "liking" a student outside the classroom. *Hofstra Labor Employment Law Journal*, *30*(1), 263−308.

boyd, D. (2006). Friends, friendsters, and MySpace Top 8: Writing community into being on social network sites. *First Monday*, *11*(12). Retrieved from ⟨http://www.firstmonday.org/issues/issue11_12/boyd/⟩ (accessed 18.01.15).

boyd, D. M., & Ellison, N. B. (2007). Social network sites: Definition, history, and scholarship. *Journal of Computer-Mediated Communication*, *13*(1), 210−230.

Carver A. (2005). Tim Berners-Lee: Weaving a semantic web. Retrieved from 〈http://www.cbpp.uaa.alaska.edu/afef/weaving%20the%20web-tim_bernerslee.htm〉 (accessed 18.01.15).

Cook, H. L. (2016). #Liability: Avoiding the Lanham Act and the right of publicity on social media. *The University of Chicago Law Review, 83*(1), 457–502.

Fowler S. (September 20, 2017). *Teacher fired after racist Facebook post.* USA Today. Retrieved from https://www.msn.com/en-us/news/us/teacher-fired-after-racist-facebook-post/ar-AAsguk4 (accessed 18.01.15).

Freedom House. (2017). *Manipulating social media to undermine democracy: Freedom on the net 2017.* Retrieved from 〈https://freedomhouse.org/sites/default/files/FOTN_2017_Final.pdf〉 (accessed 17.12.15).

Fuchs, C. (2017). *Social media: A critical introduction.* Thousand Oaks, CA: Sage.

Haythornthwaite, C. (2005). Social networks and Internet connectivity effects. *Information, Communication and Society, 8*(2), 125–147.

Jeske, D., & Shultz, K. S. (2016). Using social media content for screening in recruitment and selection: pros and cons. *Work, Employment, and Society, 30*(3), 535–546.

Lam, H. (2016). Social media dilemmas in the employment context. *Employee Relations, 38*(3), 420–437.

Martin, C. (August 3, 2011). *Law restricts student-teacher Facebook contact.* Columbia Tribune. Retrieved from 〈http://www.columbiatribune.com/b8e3f768-0dd3-5b85-b9d1-81236d1f2c50.html〉 (accessed 17.09.15).

Mathews, B. (2007). Online social networking. In N. Courtney (Ed.), *Library 2.0 and beyond: Innovative technologies and tomorrow's user* (pp. 75–90). Westport, CT: Libraries Unlimited.

Ouirdi, M. E., El Ouirdi, A., Sergers, J., & Henderickx, E. (2014). Social media conceptualization and taxonomy: A Lasswellian framework. *Journal of Creative Communications, 9*(2), 107–126.

Pew Research Center. (2009). *Pew Internet & American life project parent/teen cell phone survey [Data file and code book].* Retrieved from 〈http://www.ropercenter.uconn.edu/ipoll-database/〉 (accessed 17.09.15).

Pew Research Center. (2016). *Share of adults in the United States who use the Internet in 2016, by educational background.* In Statista—The Statistics Portal. Retrieved from 〈https://libproxy.library.unt.edu:9076/statistics/327138/internet-penetration-usa-education/〉 (accessed 18.01.15).

Rosen, A. (2017). *Giving you more characters to express yourself.* Retrieved from 〈https://blog.twitter.com/official/en_us/topics/product/2017/Giving-you-more-characters-to-express-yourself.html〉 (accessed 18.01.15).

Scott, S. V., & Orlikowski, W. J. (2012). Reconfiguring relations of accountability: Materialization of social media in the travel sector. *Accounting, Organizations and Society, 37*(1), 26–40.

Sloan, L., & Quan-Haase, A. (Eds.), (2017). *The SAGE handbook of social media research methods.* Thousand Oaks, CA: Sage.

Statista. (2018). *Most popular social networks worldwide as of January 2018, ranked by number of active users (in millions).* Retrieved from 〈https://www.statista.com/statistics/272014/global-social-networks-ranked-by-number-of-users/〉 (accessed 18.01.15).

Stelter, B. (2017). *ESPN says it accepts Jemele Hill's apology after anti-Trump tweets.* Retrieved from 〈http://money.cnn.com/2017/09/13/media/jemele-hill-espn-white-house/index.html〉 (accessed 17.09.15).

Twenge, J. M. (2017). Have smartphones destroyed a generation? *Atlantic, 320*(2), 58–65.

Warnick, B. R., Bitters, T. A., Falk, T. M., & Kim, S. H. (2016). Social media use and teacher ethics. *Educational Policy, 30*(5), 771–795.

FURTHER READING

Breed, E. (2013). Creating a social media policy: What we did, what we learned. *Information Today, 27*(2). Retrieved from ⟨http://www.infotoday.com/mls/mar13/Breed--Creating-a-Social-Media-Policy.shtml⟩ (accessed 18.01.15).

Charoensukmongkol, P. (2014). Effects of support and job demands on social media use and work outcomes. *Computers in Human Behavior, 36,* 340−349.

Gaudin, S. (February 13, 2017). *Google lets users get social with Maps.* Computerworld. Retrieved from ⟨https://www.computerworld.com/article/3169564/social-media/google-lets-users-get-social-with-maps.html⟩ (accessed 17.09.15).

Heid, M. (n.d., 2017). You asked: Is social media Making Me Miserable? *Time Magazine.* Retrieved from ⟨http://time.com/collection/guide-to-happiness/4882372/social-media-facebook-instagram-unhappy/⟩ (accessed 17.09.15).

Shakya, H. B., & Christakis, N. A. (2017). Association of Facebook use with compromised well-being: a longitudinal study. *American Journal of Epidemiology, 185*(3), 203−211.

Stoller, E. (2017). *Guidelines and policy: Social media at your university.* Retrieved from ⟨https://www.insidehighered.com/blogs/student-affairs-and-technology/guidelines-and-policy-social-media-your-university⟩ (accessed 18.01.15).

CHAPTER 2

Libraries and Social Media

Figure 2.1 Student browsing digital tablets.

2.1 HOW LIBRARIES ARE USING SOCIAL MEDIA

King (2012) remarked that library staff use social media for many of the same reasons as businesses. These reasons include listening, communicating, answering, sharing news and information, and being active online. King argues, "listening is the foundation of library social media presence" (p. 23). Listening allows library staff to understand the perspectives of the community members they serve. Searching social media for the library's city, state, or even the library itself can provide a snapshot of the community's culture, climate, and trends. If comments are specifically related to the library, improvements can be made where necessary.

King (2012) further notes that communicating and answering are related to listening. Like businesses, once librarians have an idea of the culture, trends, and climate, they can begin responding to customer questions and concerns. This helps the library build a relationship with the community.

King (2012) reminds readers that the interactive aspect of social media is significant because it allows librarians to converse directly with patrons. They connect with the library's social media account because they want to know more and most likely "like" the library for what it offers.

Growing Your Library Career with Social Media
DOI: https://doi.org/10.1016/B978-0-08-102411-9.00002-9

Because patrons are willing to stay connected, it is important for librarians to show interest in them by answering their questions. For example, a patron may ask their "friend" a question that can be answered by a librarian if they see it. Answering these questions can clear up any misconceptions that may arise from patrons receiving incorrect information online.

Social media presents the perfect opportunity for libraries to share new information. Libraries post events, news about new services, and information about the resources that are available. According to King (2012), it is not uncommon to find pictures related to libraries posted on Flicker, Twitter, and Facebook. When library staff share information online, it is easier for patrons to understand the personalities of the individuals who work in the library and how they can provide services. This makes the staff more accessible and approachable. King (2012) further argues that when library social media accounts are monitored and interactive, it makes them "come alive." This is an aspect of customer service that makes visiting the library and following its social media account worthwhile for community members.

King (2012) describes some of the social media tools libraries use to support their "digital branches" and how they are used.

- YouTube: Can be used to publish and share introduction videos for services and tours of the buildings.
- Foursquare: Helps people discover the best places to visit and share where they are currently visiting. This is a good marketing tool for libraries.
- Goodreads: Allows the creation of virtual book clubs and lets people talk about what they are reading.
- Pinterest: Can be employed to create a virtual scrapbook of web pages. A "board" or page can be set up to share various aspects of the library and resources with patrons.
- Google Plus: Provides another platform on which content can be posted, and online communities can be built.

King (2012) touches on how libraries are also using social media to train new librarians. Hagman and Carleton (2014) elaborate on this prospect. They note that establishing a social media presence requires a significant commitment and resources. This is because social media requires consistent monitoring and needs someone to build an audience and properly communicate with that audience. Moreover, social media changes frequently as more services are added. This requires the person who monitors the social media account for any library to stay up-to-date with the changes that are being made.

Librarians at the academic libraries of Ohio State (Hagman & Carleton, 2014) agree with King (2012), in that having a social media presence helps librarians and patrons build relationships, market resources, and events, and collect feedback. But managing these responsibilities is a large undertaking that can be a challenge or an opportunity. The opportunity comes in the form of a platform through which it is possible to teach student "employees" workplace skills and create a bond with the librarians. Embracing student employees as part of the communication network for social media has enabled the Ohio University Libraries to continually embrace new social media networks and maintain the content placed on these networks. The library uses paid student positions to develop Pinterest boards, write blogs, post pictures, and Tweet about various collections. Hagman and Carleton share many benefits related to using students to create content for social media accounts. These benefits include having a better understanding of student information needs, developing separate streams of communication that would not be possible without the assistance of students, monitoring blogs and social media to assess trends, and accessing research-based feedback about the norms related to social media networks (Box 2.1).

BOX 2.1 Can you provide an example of how you have used social media for work?

Greg Hardin—At Texas Woman's University (TWU), another librarian and I spearheaded the social media for the library. We wrote up a proposal and our work was featured in the Texas Library Journal.

We had a YouTube channel, a Twitter, Instagram, and a Facebook account. I think right now they probably still have Pinterest, a blog, and Instagram. I think we decided that it was at the point in time where a lot of students were leaving Twitter and Facebook and just going strictly to Instagram. And we wanted to be mindful of that. We wanted to speak for the same organization (TWU), but we wanted to have a different flavor or voice. We wanted to be intentional about using a particular platform and what it was saying. I think the Instagram was a lot lighter, fun, friendly, and humorous. We used Twitter for a lot of announcements, database downtimes, schedule changes, and just being informative. We also cross-posted. If an announcement went out on Twitter, it was on the other networks too.

Conversely, student employees benefit from developing the social media presence of libraries. Creating the content for social media helps students build their research skills. They are responsible for curating appropriate content and synthesizing it into a format that is helpful to patrons. Students learn about collaboration and appropriate communication practices. These skills are valuable for multiple work environments, including libraries. Finally, contributing to the university is personally rewarding to students. Showcasing resources, events, and the library gives students a tangible example of work that they can enjoy sharing with their friends and families.

Brookbank (2015) describes the feedback that academic libraries can receive from students. Brookbank recalls that academic libraries were initially apprehensive about adopting social media. However, using social media has now become commonplace and Brookbank suggests that libraries should adopt social media platforms according to the needs of their patrons. This requires libraries to frequently evaluate social media channels. For example, Brookbank noticed that the Facebook page for the library where she worked did not enjoy the same prominence among Facebook users as it had when the page was initially developed. The number of Facebook fans indicated that the page was only reaching a fraction of the campus community. As a result, a survey was conducted to determine how students were using social media.

Brookbank's results revealed that Facebook was still relevant to her students. The popularity of Facebook among students was followed by Pinterest and Instagram (second place), and Twitter (third place). While Brookbank's study revealed that Facebook was still a good way for the library to communicate with students, students were not looking at the library's social media feed for funny or trendy videos. Instead, they were looking at the feed for announcements, library hours, and information about events. Results also indicated that students differentiated between the information they sought on different social media feeds. For example, Twitter may have been a platform for finding news, while Instagram could be used for socializing. This suggests that one should not rely on one type of social media to communicate. Like Hagman and Carleton (2014), Brookbank suggests that librarians should endeavor to stay up-to-date on the types of social media that is available and their associated uses.

Examples of using social media are also provided by school librarians. Jonker (2014) is a serial explorer of social media platforms. At one point, while confident that his library was connected to the community, he looked for an opportunity to go beyond the traditional means of communication. This is where social media came in. Utilizing social media allows Jonker to expand his professional development leads, thus improving his professional skills. Jonker explains that library and education associations provide access to websites and conferences. Yet, social media offers instant gratification. One can get online anytime and converse with an expert who can answer a query.

Jonker has a system for using social media. He categorizes channels as either single or multipurpose. Single-purpose platforms are defined as those that can only fulfil one task. According to Jonker, single-purpose platforms include Instagram for sharing photos and Vines for sharing videos. Multipurpose platforms can be used to complete several tasks. Facebook and Twitter are both good for distributing pictures, videos, and writing opinions about topics. Jonker recommends librarians try using a multipurpose platform first because one platform may take care of all of their needs. This will help users to complete numerous tasks.

Jonker likes social media because of the diverse content that is available online. He strategically follows accounts that can offer him advice about the latest professional trends. One account is that of the American Library Association, which shares news about its own activities and those of other relevant organizations. Jonker is a frequent follower of authors and illustrators. He also uses social media for tasks such as asking patron questions, posting pictures from events, making announcements, posting student guidelines, and coordinating content with colleagues.

Although Jonker does not like to have a lot of social media accounts, he offers valuable advice for librarians who use social media. This advice is that your favorite social media platform may not be the place your audience visits the most. Therefore, learning how to use an automated service, such as If This Then That (IFTTT), can make using multiple platforms easier. For example, IFTTT will post Flickr photos of events to Twitter.

In an age when libraries are being examined for their worth, it is crucial to get responses from the public about what services and programs might be implemented. King (2015) recommends that librarians use social media to crowdsource ideas—if communities feel like they have been consulted and that their suggestions have been taken on board, it is more likely that they will utilize the resulting services and programs. Plus, social media feedback can be instantaneous; for example, websites such as Yelp. com make it easy for patrons to share their perceptions of their library visits. In addition, the Google Maps app now has a social feature that allows users to create lists of places they like with links on how their followers can access them (Gaudin, 2017). The practice of "sharing" places has grown in popularity because people trust the opinions of their friends and will frequent a place that their friends like. Hence, social media offers opportunities for marketing libraries and developing professional development skills that are too beneficial for librarians to ignore.

2.2 A STUDY OF LIBRARIANS' PERSPECTIVES ON SOCIAL MEDIA FOR CAREER DEVELOPMENT

Social media has grown increasingly popular. Numerous books have been written about how social media can be used to market library services (Koontz & Mon, 2014; Solomon, 2013). However, very little research has been conducted to determine how librarians are using social media for professional development, branding, and meeting career needs. Much of the research that has examined social media and librarians has been conducted outside of the United States. In addition, social capitalist theorists have indicated that social media is a means for developing and utilizing connections for career advancement (Benson, Morgan, & Filippaios, 2014). Librarians obviously see the value of using social media for marketing libraries. Yet there is a question surrounding how librarians, as information professionals and experts, go beyond library marketing to actively develop their careers through social media channels. It is frequently asserted that the profession of a librarian is not valued. Rebranding librarians via social media has the potential to make a difference in terms of how the profession is perceived and provide librarians with broader career opportunities.

Of the research that has been completed to date, Vanwynsberghe, Boudry, and Verdegem (2011) examined public librarians' readiness for using social media to promote library services. They determined that the use of social media is an information literacy skill and that librarians need to learn how to implement best practices. Social media literacy is defined as "the access to social media applications, the knowledge, skills, attitudes and self-efficacy of individuals to (appropriately) use social media applications and to analyze, evaluate, share and create social media content" (Vanwynsberghe et al., 2011, p. 31). Hence, it is suggested that social media use is a competency that all librarians need to master.

When studying academic librarians' use of social media, Zohoorian-Fooladia and Abrizah (2014) found that the participants in their study were motivated to use social media for feedback, managerial tasks, and promoting library services. However, their lack of confidence in their ability to use social media was one of the reasons they were not using it more. In describing flipped lessons, Smith (2015) identified various social media platforms, such as YouTube, that school librarians use for instructional design. While school librarians are using these tools to engage with their students and school communities, there has been very little examination of how school librarians employ these tools for professional development. A rare example of such a study was provided via research that was conducted by Moreillon (2015). Moreillon concluded that Twitter was helpful for building personal learning networks and as a vehicle for professional development. However, there are not sufficient studies to support Moreillon's findings. Furthermore, Moreillon was not able to identify a study that examines the basic competencies of librarians as a population. After reviewing studies such as the ones identified in this brief review, a gap that became evident was information about how librarians use social media as a professional platform to advance their careers.

To examine the research gap, an exploratory study was conducted by utilizing a self-administered online survey to examine social media as a variable in the career development of librarians. Invitations for the study were posted on librarian listservs and sent to the email addresses of academic librarians. The survey contained an open- and closed-ended questions designed to determine how often librarians participate in professional development, their involvement with online personal learning networks (PLNs), their daily use of social media, and their perceptions of social media as a viable professional development option. The survey was implemented using the software Qualtrics. IBM SPSS Statistics was used for descriptive statistical analysis. The open-ended question was coded into themes using the qualitative analysis software NVivo.

2.2.1 Study Participants

A total of 173 academic librarians participated. The study was conducted between August and November of 2017. Many of the participants were female (76.9%). The remaining participants were male (23.1%). One participant did not share details of his or her gender. A total of 95.4% of the participants had a degree in librarianship. The majority of the participants were between 35 and 44 years old. The remaining participants were 25—34 years old (28.9%), 45—54 years old (22.0%), 55—64 years old (11.0%), and 65—74 years old (4.6%). The participants had varying years of professional experience. Most of the participants had 6—10 years of experience (25.4%). The rest indicated their level of experience was 1—5 years (23.1%), 21 years or more (22.5%), 11—15 years (13.9%), 16—20 years (11.6%), and 1—11 months (3.5%).

2.2.2 Study Results

Because the study was about how librarians use social media for professional development, it was important to ask how often the participants attended professional development training. Professional development was an integral part of the participants' professional lives. However, the librarians who were surveyed as part of this study did not attend professional development as much as anticipated by the researcher. The reasons for this could include a lack of personnel to cover the participants so that they could attend training and a lack of money to fund professional development. It is also possible that the participants who did not attend professional development courses (9.2%) were simply not interested in them. Many of the participants (22.5%) attended professional development courses at least five or more times a year. A significant number of the people who completed the survey indicated that they attended professional development three times a year (18.5%), twice a year (20.2%), or once a year (19.7%). The rest of the participants disclosed that they attended professional development four times a year (9.8%).

An online personal learning network can help professionals to both discover and create new professional development opportunities. When asked if social media was part of their daily routine, the participants noted that they frequently used social media. Most participants (79.2%) either strongly agreed or agreed that social media was part of their daily lives. The remaining participants were neutral (9.2%) or strongly disagreed or disagreed (11.5%) that social media was part of their daily lives. According to the participants, most (68.8%) had an online personal learning network. For this study, the online personal learning network was defined to include people the participants knew personally and people and organizations the participants followed online to enhance their careers. Also, most of the participants either agreed or strongly agreed that they felt out of touch if they did not log in to their social media accounts for a while (55.5%). Other participants disagreed or strongly disagreed with this statement (24.3%).

Some of the participants answered that they were neutral (20.2%). Social media acquaintances were often a part of the participants' professional lives. For instance, when asked if social media friends were part of their online personal learning network, 79% of the participants selected yes and 21% selected no. The participants had many social media friends. 27.2% of the participants stated they had more than 400 friends. The two other categories for the number of online friends were 101–150 (12.7%) and 301–400 (12.7%).

As expected, social media was an integral part of the participants' lives. For instance, 79.2% of participants noted that social media was a part of their daily routine. The responses varied greatly when the participants were asked if they attended online professional development offered by individuals and organizations outside of their job. The largest percentage of the participants (22.5%) noted that they attended this type of professional development five or more times a year. The remaining participants answered twice a year (20.2%), once a year (19.7%), three times a year (18.5%), four or more times a year (9.8%), or never (9.2%). Overall, most of the participants (90.8%) found online professional development relevant as indicated by their attendance.

In the responses, 61.3% of the participants noted that social media was compatible with their professional development needs. In addition, 71.1% responded that they agreed or strongly agreed that using social media for professional purposes was a good idea. While the majority of participants perceived the use of social media for professional purposes to generally be a good idea, most (61.8%) of the participants further agreed or strongly agreed that using social media was fun or that they liked working with social media (60.7%).

A great number of the participants were comfortable with using social media. When asked if they were apprehensive about using it, 71.7% indicated they were not, 28.3% were neutral, and 15.0% agreed or strongly agreed. The majority of the participants (78%) were not intimidated by the prospect of using social media, 13.9% were neutral, and 8.3% (or 14) of the 173 participants stated they were intimidated. In addition, most of the participants (68.2%) were not hesitant about using social media because they were concerned about making mistakes online.

At this point, the survey focused on the librarians who were using social media for professional development through an online personal learning network. The participants were asked if they had an online personal learning network, of which, just 68.8% (or 119) of the participants disclosed that they did. To determine how important it was to communicate with the personal learning network, respondents who had established a network were asked if they felt out of touch when they did not communicate with members of their personal learning network for a while. A total of 51.3% of the participants agreed or strongly agreed that they did feel out of touch. However, 25.2% were neutral, and 23.5% disagreed or strongly agreed. Of the participants who answered they had an online personal learning network, 65.5% agreed or strongly agreed that they would feel disappointed if they did not have an online personal learning network with which to interact. However, interacting with an online personal learning network was not always part of the participants' every-day lives. For example, 16.0% of the participants strongly agreed, and 35.3% agreed that their personal learning network was a part of their everyday lives, while 22.7% of participants were neutral and 26% dis-agreed or strongly disagreed.

The participants were asked about their favorite social media tools for remaining up-to-date professionally. Responses were received from 87.9% of the participants. The most frequent responses were Twitter, Facebook, LinkedIn, Listservs, and Instagram. See Fig. 2.2 for the complete list of frequencies in terms of the types of social media tools used.

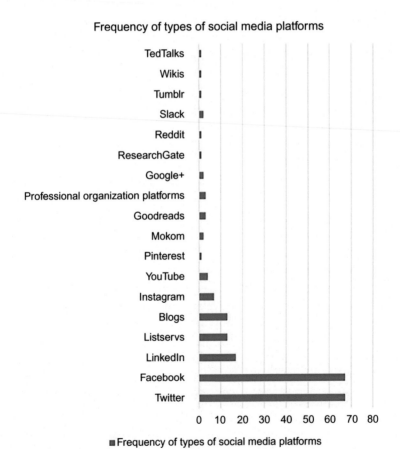

Figure 2.2 Frequency of types of social media platforms.

2.3 DISCUSSION AND CONCLUSION

In conclusion, academic librarians are very active on social media. They know and understand the value of social media for marketing libraries and personal use. The participants' favorite platforms include Facebook and Twitter. While they are active, they are not fully utilizing social media for professional development or branding beyond the use of Twitter for chats or Facebook to review posts. Moreover, many of the librarians who participated in this study did not have online personal learning networks. Research notes that these networks can be effective for fulfilling the learning needs of individuals and adds a degree of personalization to the learning process (Davis, 2015; Rosenberg, Greenhalgh, Koehler, Hamilton, & Akcaoglu, 2016).

The needs of library patrons are continually evolving. This necessitates professional development on a frequent basis. Social media offers librarians an opportunity to build personal learning communities and access free online professional development opportunities. Librarians are also not marketing themselves as experts on LinkedIn like other professionals. Posting on social media on platforms, such as LinkedIn, can help to change people's perceptions of libraries and librarians. Overall, besides advertising library programs, evidence suggests that librarians are underutilizing the benefits of social media for personal branding, networking, and professional development.

2.4 CHAPTER CHALLENGES

1. Look at the websites of three different libraries at which you would like to work. How are the librarians using social media on those websites? What ideas do you have in terms of how the use of social media on those websites can be improved?
2. Look at the skills of the librarians who are using social media for a job that you would like. Review their vitae to see how they market themselves. What type of social media presence do they have? What skills do you currently have? What skills do you currently need? How would you describe yourself in an interview so that you can appear to be an attractive candidate in comparison to these librarians?

REFERENCES

Benson, V., Morgan, S., & Filippaios, F. (2014). Social career management: Social media and employability skills gap. *Computers in Human Behavior, 30*, 519–525.

Brookbank, E. (2015). So much social media, so little time: Using student feedback to guide academic library social media strategy. *Journal of Electronic Resources Librarianship, 27*(4), 232–247. Available from https://doi.org/10.1080/1941126X.2015.1092344.

Davis, K. (2015). Teachers' perceptions of Twitter for professional development. *Disability and Rehabilitation, 37*(17), 1551–1558.

Gaudin, S. (February 13, 2017). Google lets users get social with maps. *Computerworld*. Retrieved from < https://www.computerworld.com/article/3169564/social-media/google-lets-users-get-social-with-maps.html > Accessed 17.09.15.

Hagman, J., & Carleton, J. (2014). Better together: Collaborating with students on library social media. *Public Services Quarterly, 10*(3), 238–244. Available from https://doi.org/10.1080/15228959.2014.931207.

Jonker, T. (2014). I tried, I 'liked,' I shared: How Travis Jonker handles social media. *School Library Journal Online*. Retrieved from ⟨http://www.slj.com/2014/10/technology/i-tried-i-liked-i-shared-so-many-social-media-outlets-so-little-time-heres-one-approach/⟩ Accessed 18.02.01.

King, D. L. (2015). *Managing your library's social media channels*. Chicago, IL: ALA TechSource.

King, D. L. (2012). Social media. *Library Technology Reports, 48*(6), 23–27.

Koontz, C., & Mon, L. (2014). *Marketing and social media: A guide for libraries, archives, and museums*. Lanham, MD: Rowman & Littlefield.

Moreillon, J. (2015). #schoollibrarians tweet for professional development: A netnographic case study of #txlchat. *School Libraries Worldwide, 21*(2), 127–137.

Rosenberg, J. M., Greenhalgh, S. P., Koehler, M. J., Hamilton, E. R., & Akcaoglu, M. (2016). An investigation of state educational twitter hashtags (SETHs) as affinity spaces. *E-Learning and Digital Media, 13*(1–2), 24–44.

Solomon, L. (Ed.), (2013). *The librarian's nitty-gritty guide to social media*. Chicago, IL: American Library Association.

Smith, D. (2015). Tools and tips for flipped lesson development. *Texas Library Journal, 91*(2), 54–55.

Vanwynsberghe, H., Boudry, E., & Verdegem, P. (2011). Mapping social media literacy: Towards a conceptual framework. Retrieved from ⟨http://emsoc.be/wp-content/uploads/2012/01/emsoc-WP2-MICT-deliverable1_14.pdf⟩ Accessed 17.10.17.

Zohoorian-Fooladi, N., & Abrizah, A. (2014). Academic librarians and their social media presence: a story of motivations and deterrents. *Information Development, 30*(2), 159–171.

CHAPTER 3

Social Media and Personal Branding

Figure 3.1 Personal branding on a laptop.

3.1 INTRODUCTION

There has been a growing emphasis on the importance of colleges and universities teaching students how to use social media to build social capital (Russ, 2015). Social capital refers to the relationships that one builds in society. These relationships help individuals function properly as productive members of society. Seibert, Kraimer, and Linden (2001) indicate that social capital helps professionals to successfully find career leads, identify protégés, and pinpoint resources that facilitate career development. While education can directly impact an individual's career progression, social capital is also a primary consideration that must be factored into development opportunities (Russ, 2015).

The movie, *The Circle* (Bregman, Goetzman, Hanks, Ponsoldt, & Ponsoldt, 2017), presents an interesting take on the pros and cons of social media. In the movie, the main character, May, initially has a temporary job, which she uses to support her parents financially. However, her friend, who is in a leadership role at a technology company, helps her to secure a permanent customer service job in the organization at which she works.

As May settles into her job, she finds that the social media context of the workplace becomes an integral part of her own personal and

Growing Your Library Career with Social Media
DOI: https://doi.org/10.1016/B978-0-08-102411-9.00003-0
27

professional lives, and those of the people she loves. May is initially apprehensive about using social media; however, after gentle persuasion from her coworkers, she finds that she enjoys being a part of "the circle's" online community, through which she engages in more social interaction in the physical world.

Later in the movie, she reflects on how her life has evolved and how she has developed connections with people all over the world . . . connections from which she is now unable to disconnect. She has become reliant upon the continual communication and camaraderie that characterize online interactions. However, through various mishaps, she comes to realize that using social media puts her own privacy at risk and that of the people with whom she interacts. The movie positions social media as an ever-evolving Pandora's box. While it can be employed for the common good to help society grow into a global community, it also has a dark side that is ignored at one's peril.

While *The Circle* is a work of fiction, its underlying messages have implications in the real world. How much information can employers access about employees via their social media profiles? Should employees be mandated to use social media for work purposes? Should our use of social media at work cross the line into our personal lives? When do we have the right to refuse to use our social media profiles for work-related activities?

In *The Circle*, May proactively employs social media to build her brand. At the beginning of the movie, she is perceived to be a "guppy," someone who is at the outset of her career. However, by the end of the movie, her popularity has significantly increased due to her social networking activities. As her "friends" watch and chat with her, their responses to her social media activities validate her as a professional. She progresses from a novice to an expert whose opinion is valued and sought after. Although May is a fictional character, in the real world, many people use social media channels to validate themselves as experts, enhance their popularity, and build their professional personal brands. Let's look at how personal branding and social media can help you.

3.2 WHAT IS PERSONAL BRANDING?

Although social media is one of the most commonly used tools for developing a personal brand, Llopis (2013) asserts that it is not the only component of personal branding. According to Llopis, personal branding is a part of leadership development. It is a process that requires an ongoing commitment through which the brand image is nurtured on a continual basis. Because personal branding is an ongoing evolution, you need to begin with a distinct set of goals in mind. What is the primary objective that underpins your personal branding activities? How will this affect you within and outside the workplace?

Llopis (2013) further asserts that the personal brand needs to represent the characteristics, skills, knowledge, and abilities that set the individual apart from everyone else. What can you offer to other people that they cannot get elsewhere? What is your area of expertise? For Llopis, personal branding is not necessarily about telling everyone why you are important and bragging about your accomplishments; it is a way to serve as a role model for people who need advice. It involves accepting the responsibility to engage other people with valuable information that will help them successfully achieve their goals. In this way, personal branding requires a level of accountability. You must be willing to assume high standards for the image and content you deliver.

Because personal branding requires the creation of content and an identity, you need to consider it as an asset that demands constant protection. Assets need to be monitored, managed, and nurtured. Consider yourself as part of the stock market. Your value can fluctuate depending on how the public views you as a commodity (Box 3.1).

According to Llopis, personal branding requires a strong sense of self-awareness. People who engage in personal branding activities need to be explicitly aware of the image they are projecting when they attend meetings, present at conferences, write articles, and post on social media. Every single action you take gives other people insights into your knowledge, character, goals, potential, and professionalism. Are you leaving people with a positive impression? Are your actions reflective of how you

BOX 3.1 What tips do you have for building your personal brand with social media?

Greg Hardin—*I would say be very intentional, and thoughtful about almost every move you make. Don't be afraid to experiment or try out some new things. But do look at the outcomes. Ask yourself, "Okay, did that work?" If you put out a series of things, on Twitter or a blog, is it getting a reaction? Is it a positive reaction? Then, also, I think probably having a personal slant is good.*

want people to perceive you? Do you believe that if you asked people about who you are and what you stand for, they would be able to answer the question in a way that is aligned with where you want to be in your career? According to Llopis, if you answer no to any of these questions, you need to work on creating an image that is more closely aligned with your objectives.

Quast (2013) contends that creating a personal brand is much like developing a brand for a product. Hypothetically, each product that is on the shelf in a store is different from the next in some way, shape, or form. The same differentiations are needed when one develops a personal brand to set themselves apart from competitors. On this basis, Quast observes that a significant problem people who are seeking to develop personal brands experience concerns the level of research they perform to learn about other people in the field. She recommends following six steps on the path to personal brand development:

1. Identify goals and objectives
2. Do research
3. Decide attributes
4. Assess current image
5. Develop a plan
6. Manage the growing brand

Let's look at a scenario that involves the first five of these steps for Lisa, a library school student who is about to graduate.

1. **Identify goals and objectives.** Lisa anticipates that she will have two full semesters left in library school. She has been working in the campus library using a special program to acclimatize students to the work of a librarian. Some of her responsibilities for this program have included developing a social media presence for the library that show-cases its archives related to the life of a local activist. She has been offering tours of the collection, interacting with faculty members, and leading local expeditions. She feels this experience is important for her goals of becoming an archivist and special collections librarian. Along the way, her role has taught her some important lessons. She believes this information will be helpful to future students and budding special collection librarians. She would like to use her experiences and knowledge of procedures to market herself as an expert, participate in conferences, and land her first position.

2. **Perform research.** Lisa begins to engage in research to learn about other people who are working in a similar position to that she wishes

to secure. She reviews their social media profiles, visits their biographies on their library websites, and reads relevant job descriptions to determine the skills that are pertinent to the position she wants to acquire. She realizes that she is already performing many of the tasks that are required for the position. However, there are some additional areas in which she would like to gain some experience before applying for relevant jobs.

3. **Decide attributes.** Lisa decides that she wants to develop a strong reputation for her archiving skills. In addition to landing her first position as a special collections librarian, she wants to deliver workshops and conference presentations through which she shares her expertise on her topic. It is important for her to be perceived as a knowledgeable professional instead of a newcomer to the field. Eventually, she would like to write books and develop a YouTube channel to supplement her income.

4. **Assess current image.** Lisa begins to assess her own image and questions what she needs to do to be regarded as an expert. While she posts for the library and delivers tours, she is not widely known beyond her own campus. She also does not have a social media presence separate from the work she posts online via the library page or for her personal interactions with family and friends. She begins to think about the networking events she can attend during conferences. She also notes the attire she wears at these conferences and the pictures she has posted online. At the moment, they show her as a fun-loving college student. While these images are part of her digital footprint, she would like to start posting professional images and infographics that reflect her as a change agent and knowledgeable professional.

5. **Develop a plan.** Lisa develops a plan that spans a range of activities. She talks with her boss and requests that some of the tasks she is completing at work are broadened. She also begins to attend some of the professional development workshops that are offered by the American Library Association and its affiliates. During these classes, she meets many new like-minded people, that is, professionals who are aspiring to become archivists and special collections librarians. In addition, she meets an instructor who becomes a valuable resource for her. She follows the instructor online along with the other people she identified as being relevant during her research process. Her plan also involves creating a social media presence of her own. This presence is separate

from the content she posts for family and friends. To separate her professional and personal images, she privatizes the accounts on which she shares personal posts. She is a busy student but resolves that she will update her blog at least every two weeks. Occasionally, she will interview other people to enhance the materials on her blog.

The personal branding process that Lisa has engaged in is not new. Khedher (2014) credits Tom Peters with commercializing the term personal branding in a 1997 article called "The Brand Called You." Since the Internet was very much in a growth stage at this point, Peters was not referring to self-promotion online. He was addressing how individuals present themselves and conduct business. Peters asserted that each person is the chief executive officer of his or her own company, "Me Inc.," which has its own brand called "You." To thrive, people must market themselves in a similar way to how companies market their products and services. They should not allow labels such as "student" or "junior," to stop them from projecting themselves as professionals. Remaining within these confines will only serve to hinder progress and stop you from dreaming about your possibilities.

Peters encouraged everyone to think of themselves as a free agent who needs to establish a niche. Establishing a niche helps people to limit the opportunities they seek. This is important so that they don't try to assume every responsibility they are presented with. By narrowing down the areas of specialization, as a free agent, you can establish yourself as an expert in what matters to you. Being an expert makes one marketable, primed to pursue training that fits their specialization, and an expert worthy of attention. As such, Peters remarks that a brand value acts as an indication of the quality of resources that one can offer.

When examining competitors, such as other people in the job market, people you admire, and experts in your field, bear in mind that you ultimately want to surpass their success. Consider the qualities they have that will suit you. Then think about what you know and have done recently that sets you apart from other people. These are strengths that should be emphasized during personal branding activities. Peters pointed out that Nordstrom stands out among its competitors because the store emphasizes personalized service. This personalized service is perceived as a benefit to customers. When thinking about your personal brand, identify the benefit you offer to others. What is the benefit of contacting you for your services? Think about the problems you can solve for other people. Think about how your approach to solving these problems is different from that adopted by other people (i.e., your competitors).

Let's look at the difference in the way people approach problems within the context of Lisa's situation. Lisa knows that Jane Doe works in an academic library and has become well known for the humanities research guides she creates. Jane posts her research guides online so that they are readily available. She is often invited to conferences to talk about the material she has produced and to share her expertise. The difference between Jane and Lisa is that Lisa has a degree in humanities. Not only can she create the same type of guide as those generated by Jane, but she can also essentially deliver a lecture about specific time-eras, and her work is frequently published in journals. Lisa's guides are embedded with multimedia resources, such as videos, that she has created from her personal knowledge and podcasts, during which she invites experts from the field to talk about various topics. In addition to creating guides about the humanities, she has established an audience of humanities enthusiasts and researchers due to her content knowledge. In addition to respecting her content knowledge about humanities, people like the way she has designed her mini-documentaries and podcasts and want to learn about the process she follows to create them. She has established a niche within which her skills are perceived to be superior to those of others.

According to Peters, in addition to identifying a niche, one must also find a way to market themselves to others. Lisa could have the best guides in the world, but if she wants to reach a greater audience beyond her immediate followers, she will have to find a way to tell people why her guides and services are so important and unique. It doesn't matter how great you are at what you do if you are unable to deliver your messages to other people.

Peters (1997) acknowledges that people do not have a huge marketing budget like large companies. He presented six affordable and realistic methods of teaching others about your skills and enhancing perceptions of your professional skills:

- Volunteer to help interesting people.
- Teach a class at a community college as part of an adult education program.
- Start your own company and teach classes.
- If you are working at a company, moonlight at another organization to demonstrate your skills and learn more.
- Become a speaker or panel member at conferences.
- Offer workshops at conferences.

Peters suggests that everything about a person communicates their personal brand. For example, communication in meetings should be well articulated, short, and meaningful. Emails should suggest that you have a strong command of written language. Phone conversations need to be professional at all times. Business cards should be well designed. Attire needs to look polished. Information that is posted online should communicate that you have a command of technology. Even what you decide not to do communicates your brand. For example, if you are invited to attend a panel on digital citizenship at a conference, and you choose not to accept, people will form the opinion that you lack experience in digital citizenship.

Word of mouth can also have a significant impact on how people perceive you. It is for this reason that it is important to nurture your contacts. You need people to say good things about what you have to offer. Think carefully before you act. Your reputation is your power. Protect and grow it. Peters suggests that one can grow their reputation by taking power trips that are unobtrusive and positive. Look for opportunities to shine. This may include taking on tasks that may be relatively mundane. You can also be the team problem solver. Consider the types of deliverables you can offer and how these may extend your bragging rights (Box 3.2).

BOX 3.2 How can librarians use social media to get noticed for jobs?

Greg Hardin—Think about what your niche area is. All of us should have a certain area that we're striving to be an expert in or the best we can be. Concentrate on that area. If you are just talking about academic librarians on social media and try to be the best academic librarian, you are going to get lost in the sea of all the other academic librarians. You could narrow it down to the first-year experience or English composition instruction. What are you doing that you have experience in? How can you share that experience to help other people?

Preplan your social media presence. I have seen a lot of people apply for jobs and put their social media links on their CV. When you go back to look at their presence, it either exploded in the past month or, it only started in the past month. You can tell that they are looking for a job and ramped their presence up just for the purpose of the job search. So, make your social media activity something that you are working on for the long run, even if it is just a little bit. Then you show history purpose, and intention. Your social media presence is something that you should take seriously. Posting on social media is not something you should limit to the period of your job search.

(Continued)

BOX 3.2 (Continued)

Make sure that you share links to your social media account on your CV. Make it part of your header. Make it part of your cover letter. That is one thing I did with my website. I utilized it to branch out and push traffic to my Twitter, Facebook, LinkedIn, and other online accounts.

__kYmberly Keeton__—I believe that LinkedIn and having a website is the best bet. I have a digital CV too. I find that employers and potential clients have found me this way. I do not believe that Facebook is an option for employers to be searching for people for professional roles. However, I do believe that LinkedIn is taken into account and held in a higher regard than other social media platforms as it pertains to professionalism.

__Ayla Stein__—I think trying to interact and engage with conversations that are going on is probably the best way to get noticed.

3.3 USING SOCIAL MEDIA FOR PERSONAL BRANDING

If you are reading this book and questioning whether you should invest time in setting up some social media accounts, the answer is yes. Of course, you should not be reckless with social media. This is a correct process for everything. However, social media is something that should not be ignored.

Talan (2017) highlights the importance of establishing a professional brand online. Will people find you if they perform an online search for your area of expertise? Talan, an assistant professor at American University, noted that approximately 75% of browsers do not search beyond the first page of results on Google. Are you on the second page? According to Talan, professors have brands that must be marketed to enhance their visibility. In the age of sites such as Rate My Professors, you don't want the comments published on crowdsourcing sites to represent the main contribution to the ultimate perception of who you are. Personal branding enables you to control how people view your work. Moreover, branding can even increase your access to professional opportunities, including speaking engagements, networking events, and job announcements.

Regardless of whether you decide to set up social media profiles or not, if you are a professional who works with the public, it is highly likely that you are talked about somewhere online, by an individual, news outlet, or organization. The key to making a difference through social media is being proactive about how you present yourself, thereby, influencing the information people find.

Talan suggested a variety of tools for professional branding purposes. For example, if you write research articles, Google Scholar offers a way to connect with other researchers. Creating a simple "About Me" page is a convenient way to give the world a glimpse of your resume. You can also quickly and easily develop a blog using tools such as Blogger or WordPress.

Talan also suggested taking the following steps to understand your personal brand.

1. Ask people who they feel you are and what they think of your work.
2. Reflect on how effectively you create emotional connections with others.
3. Assess why you are valuable and the skills you have that set you apart from others.
4. Examine your soft and hard assets. According to Talan (2017): "Hard assets are tangible things like your typing speed, knowledge of Excel, and ability to speak a foreign language. Soft assets are things like your ability to work with others and manage your time" (para. 8).
5. Define what you want to achieve.
6. Examine the extent to which your existing brand and goals are aligned with the needs of the current market and the needs you would like to address.
7. Write down your personal brand statement. The statement embodies what you want people to believe about you and the work you offer to the world.
8. Begin using your personal brand statement, the results about what you learned about yourself, and your goals to inform what you create, share, and promote online.

Talan likens the use of social media to the equivalent of "publish or perish" … the idea in academia that if one does not publish articles to make their name or brand known, they will not earn tenure because they are not relevant in their respective field of expertise. Unlike traditional journals, social media is available to a broader audience. While traditional journals are accessible to a small percentage of the population that has access to subscriptions, social media is typically widely available with social networks having a variety of access levels from free to premium availability. Even paid social networks have some type of comment that the public can freely access.

Talan encourages readers to understand that a personal brand can change over time. Think about it. Are you the same person you were as a teenager or undergraduate student? Have you changed your career aspirations?

If you have developed over time, it is okay. Creating a personal brand is like going through a process of self-evaluation. As time goes by, you may find that you need to make changes to how you are perceived or the skills you market. For example, you may find that your library offers a new service that is in high demand. To be perceived as an expert in this service, you may need to change your brand. You may also find that you have skills that are underappreciated because your other skills are highlighted for your current positions. Sometimes, you may need to prepare for a job or career change by adapting your personal brand. If you continually market the same skills and never examine the possibilities of self-promotion, your career may become stale. Simply stated, sometimes we need to change with the times to remain relevant.

3.4 THE BENEFITS OF USING SOCIAL MEDIA TO GROW YOUR CAREER

Social media allows users to access several benefits that can help them to grow their career and understand their audiences. Some of the benefits are as follows:

1. You can learn about how people feel about various topics related to your specialty. Understanding a topic helps you to develop your own materials. By establishing a social media presence, you begin to understand the vocabulary that is associated with your area.
2. You can position yourself as an expert. Offer new insights into a subject by building on the foundation that others have provided.
3. You can grow a professional community around your interests. People use social media to find and share information that increases their visibility. Building a strong relationship with these people can turn them into your advocates in the future.
4. By using social media, you also learn more about what people need to know. What are the reoccurring topics? How can you solve the problems associated with these topics?
5. You can learn about how people feel about the services they are being offered. What competing products are available? How can you make the services and products better?

6. You can review current job postings to see the types of skills needed to get a job. See Appendix 9 for a list of organizations with websites and social media accounts that are focused on LIS job searches.

3.5 DEFINING THE PERSONAL LEARNING NETWORK (PLN)

You no longer need someone to direct you to professional development opportunities. With the access that is available to a variety of online materials through blogs, websites, and social media feeds, one can build a robust agenda for professional development without the need to pay hefty fees or to sit in a class for hours. Sure, sitting in a class can be a valuable investment. Furthermore, all the information that is available online is not always credible. However, with some creative searching and evaluating, you can determine who you want to contact to build a personal learning network (PLN) (Box 3.3).

BOX 3.3 How has social media helped you with your professional development?

Kelly Hoppe—I get advice from other librarians. For example, I had some ideas about professional development opportunities for the people in my department, but I was struggling with where to start and how to put it all together. I was just scrolling through Twitter one day, and another academic librarian Tweeted about something that she had done, and it clicked. It was kind of like, "Oh, this is sort of where I want to go with what I want to do." So, I commented explaining my questions and asked if I could connect with her via email. We connected via email, and she gave me more details about what I wanted to do.

Ayla Stein—I think it's made me much more aware of issues in librarianship, and really the broader news and pop culture and society, that I wasn't aware of previously. Social media is where I first started hearing about critical theory, critical librarianship, and critical digital humanities... all those critical theories, and intersectionality, feminism, et cetera. Of course, I'd heard about feminism, but I hadn't studied a whole lot about it in school. We didn't really talk about it very much in grad school. I think the other thing that I really like about Twitter is that you can meet people on Twitter and connect with people that you wouldn't necessarily be able to meet or connect with in real life.

For the purpose of this book, a personal learning network is a group of people organizations that you interact with to increase your knowledge on a chosen topic. Think of a PLN as part of your professional development plan. Of course, you don't need one. Still, a professional development plan is nice to have. There is nothing like having an expert at your disposal. PLNs can be face-to-face or online. Tour (2017) writes, "A current generation of technologies offers spaces for social interaction, participation, generating and distributing multimodal content, networking, collaboration, sharing, exchange and creativity" (p. 12).

It is possible to build a PLN using social media. There is plenty of useful information available that you can access when you don't have the time or the resources to attend a conference or class. In fact, sometimes you can vicariously attend a conference through social media posts without being physically present. For example, the Online Learning Consortium has an intricate social media component with ambassadors and hashtags.

In 2017, the American Association of School Librarians hosted a conference but understood that many librarians could not attend. To share the experience, each day, awards were given to the librarians that had the best social media presence. Comments were posted about sessions, and the association members that were not in attendance at the event responded with questions and comments of their own related to the trending topics. Joining an organization can give you a connection with many like-minded professionals. However, you do not need to be a member of an association to interact with its members on social media when comments are posted to the general public. You just have to know the relevant hashtags or follow an organization to see the public posts.

If you can locate someone with a robust social media presence, you can also look at who this individual is communicating with and the types of posts they are creating. Based on those posts, look for organizations and other people with whom you might connect. Follow these individuals and try liking or retweeting a couple of their posts to build up interest in your ideas.

Another idea for increasing your online PLN is to connect with the people you work with. However, this is not necessarily a preference for many professionals. For example, Sie et al. (2013) found that most of the participants in their study formed personal learning networks, with their research collaborators, friends, and colleagues outside of work. Build a private community to explore topics that are common to you. It is suggested that the network is private to separate your personal life from your professional life on social media.

Networks like Facebook and Google Plus allow you to search for interesting people and organizations to follow. Moreover, you can research which people and organizations use the hashtags that you are interested in. Remember, you can lurk on a social media network to observe what a group is doing if their posts are not private. This is useful if you are not sure that you want to join.

When studying how teachers use online PLNs, Tour (2017) found that some teachers remarked that using an online PLN provided some of the best professional development opportunities they had ever encountered. Tour noted that an online PLN offers a place to engage in conversations, participate in debates, and access answers to questions. The interesting part about online PLNs is that age is often not a factor that influences perceptions of an individual's level of knowledge about a topic (Ito, 2010). In that way, there is no pressure to feel like you have all the answers because you have the most experience on the job. Tour (2017) also noted the benefits of using the PLN at times that were most convenient. The study participants also thought of the existence of a PLN as professional coaching.

Interesting enough, Lankau and Scandura (2002) note that when mentoring exists in the workplace, people are more likely to seek personal learning. Conversely, by encouraging you to invest in your own personal learning, PLNs can also be useful when you seek another job. Certainly, developing a PLN is better than a supervisor noting that you should look for professional development or seek a mentor to help you with your work. Another benefit that Tour pointed out in relation to PLNs is that they represent an active way of learning that is reciprocal. Participants frequently share just as much knowledge as they receive (Sie et al., 2013), thus making it a fulfilling voluntary activity for everyone involved. A PLN is a place to share resources and develop collective wisdom (Box 3.4).

BOX 3.4 Why did you join Twitter?

Kelly Hoppe—Well, I knew it had been around for a while, but I was scared of it. For some reason, I felt like I was going to start uncontrollably sort of verbally vomiting all sorts of private information that I didn't want anybody to know, or I felt like somehow that people would be able to find out private information about me. I guess I just didn't understand it. I saw it being used more and more at conferences and things like that. I thought, "I have got to start doing this if I want to be the librarian that I claim to be," because all of the librarians who were at the forefront of things were using Twitter. I just kind of bit the bullet and created an account. I never looked back. I absolutely love it, and it's been amazing.

3.6 DEVELOPING YOUR PROFESSIONAL PRESENCE

Convey your life. Do you have a message that you are passionate about? Do you want to transform your career? One trait that many thought leaders share is an ability to communicate. Social media can help you to share your knowledge with the professional community. Used correctly, social media can provide you with a platform for giving back to the community and making connections with like-minded people who can help you to evolve into the professional you want to be. Employers like to see new professionals who are motivated and passionate about their profession. Social media allows us to glean information from experts and other people who have had similar experiences. What would you like to know? Share your truth while carefully absorbing the best of the knowledge that is available to you.

Before you start posting to social media, ask yourself some crucial questions:

1. To what level do you ultimately want to progress?
2. How can you change mundane work into something you find more interesting?
3. What is the *why* behind your work? (i.e., Why is it important?)
4. What potential lies ahead in your career?
5. What is your vision?

Developing and sharing your vision can breathe life into your ambitions. Use social media to share the concepts that mean the most to you with other people. It is possible for you to become a thought leader for the issues that sit within your core. You can do this because social media is an equalizing plain for those who are willing to work hard to promote their ideas. However, it is not without its downsides. For example, Heid (2018) describes how "people with anxiety or mood disorders are more likely to use social media compulsively, but that compulsive use may also promote these sorts of negative emotional states" (para.14).

If you want to use social media to brand yourself, adopt an entrepreneurial mindset. Learn to subsidize your knowledge with diverse streams of information. It is difficult to understand different viewpoints if you don't take the time to explore them. By studying multiple perspectives, you develop insights into the pros and cons of what other people are saying and can subsequently enhance your own viewpoint.

Create a team or personal learning network to support your vision. Don't let other people's notions of what your focus should be define your goals. Surround yourself with people who can complement your skills.

3.7 CREATING AN INFRASTRUCTURE

The benefit of social media is that you don't have to consistently monitor it every hour of the day. Of course, some people do. But you have work to do, right? You can step away from your computer, and your social media accounts will still work for you. However, you must create an infrastructure that can support the well-being of your career first.

Begin by identifying people on social media who you want to be like (see Appendix 8: Librarians on Twitter for a preliminary list). If you have yet to reach your desired level of success and continue to associate with people who are the same as you, you will continue to constrain yourself to a mindset that recycles the same ideas. Actively seek opportunities to interact with the people who have the attributes you want to exhibit and who have similar visions to your own; this will enhance your creativity. While the list of Librarians on Twitter presented in Appendix 8 contains details of librarians who you may want to follow, library and information science is an interdisciplinary field. It is perfectly fine to look outside the field to identify trendsetters.

It is natural to gravitate to people who are the same as you. However, when you connect with people who have different attitudes and perspectives, you challenge your own outlook and connect with your own values on a deeper level. Embrace diversity. Feed your mind with new concepts. Most importantly, create your career on your own terms; make your career meaningful (Box 3.5).

BOX 3.5 Has social media impacted your career?

Greg Hardin—I have received invitations to present and collaborate on projects through social media. Also, I would like to think that it played a part in making myself more attractive in gaining a position here at UNT. I don't necessarily have hard evidence of that, but I've been told "You're known out there." So, that's a positive.

Dr. Spencer Keralis—One of the things that it does is it connects me to a network of people who are similar, or thinking about similar topics and interested in similar causes, and who are also in similar clinical positions within the academy. Because there's a lot of us with humanities PhDs who are working in advising and libraries, and other roles that aren't necessarily what we trained for. Social media gives us a space where we can have conversations about that. I can share resources, share job postings, and promote our own scholarship. That's one of the things that's been fantastic.

(Continued)

BOX 3.5 (Continued)

You meet a lot of cool people; I've made social connections that have turned into collaborative connections. Now I am working on a quarter of a million-dollar grant proposal, with someone from another university who I've never actually met in person at another university. We got to know each other via Twitter. If you use social media strategically, and if you are not boring, it can open tremendous personal and professional connections for you.

3.8 TRENDS AND BRANDING

Match the current trends to your environment. What is the trend that will help you maximize your brand? When you recognize this trend, consider your environment and how you need to approach the trend. The trend must connect to your work environment and how you want to articulate your career aspirations. In the same vein, you don't want to embrace every trend that is around. The trends must hold meaning for you and your career.

3.9 LEARN TO FAIL

The basketball player Michael Jordan once stated, "I've missed more than 9,000 shots in my career. I've lost almost 300 games. 26 times I've been trusted to take the game-winning shot and missed. I've failed over and over and over again in my life. And that is why I succeed."

Sometimes the things that you choose to highlight on social media may attract negative feedback. Personal branding has an element of risk-taking. And the thing that differentiates leaders and changes agents from the rest of society is the ability to recognize trends, the opportunity for change, and the willingness to take calculated risks (Kouzes & Posner, 2007).

Continue to build your reputation and reinvent yourself as needed. This does not mean that you should completely change your brand every few months into a new form that is completely unlike the previous incarnation. You should actively seek opportunities to enhance the elements of who you are. Don't be afraid to abandon a path or strategy that is not working for you. Just as the eight-track tape has developed into digital downloads, you can continue to make improvements with the times. If you are not sure about the changes you need to make, get feedback from your personal learning network (PLN).

3.10 DECIDE ON YOUR NICHE

When you consider your personal branding, think about the niche you want to fulfill. From your observations, can you describe what people need? What problem can you solve? How do the problems that exist match your personal skills? How can you acquire the skills required to meet the needs of other people?

Help people to understand why their knowledge is valuable to them. People will find you valuable to the degree that your knowledge meets their immediate needs. Be careful how you invest in your branding efforts. If your efforts are not meeting the goals you have set for yourself, you should modify the idea. Measure the impact your efforts are having on your social media platforms. For example, you may wish to consider the following:

- Are your page views increasing?
- Do you have more friends?
- Are these friends adding value to your career development?
- Do you get presentation and speaking engagements if you are seeking them?
- Are you developing new ideas from your interactions?

3.11 CONCLUSION

In conclusion, developing your personal brand is just as much about knowing who you are as a professional as it is about knowing who you want to become. Personal branding is a process that can greatly improve your career and quality of life. However, to develop an effective personal brand, you need to invest time into curating your image.

Be honest with yourself about the work that needs to be done and how it can be achieved. Develop a strong foundation of people who are willing to mentor you and tell you the truth about how others may perceive you. In addition, study the individuals who have achieved success in your niche or whose careers you aspire to emulate. This can help you to assess your current strengths, weaknesses, and potential areas of growth.

3.12 CHAPTER CHALLENGES

1. Ask someone what they believe your professional brand is. Ask them how they have come to this conclusion. Based on their response,

determine if you are projecting the correct image for the brand that you want to portray.

2. Look for five leaders in your area of expertise. Examine the social media profiles and resumes of these individuals. What qualities do they have that you would like to mimic? Determine some activities that you can complete to begin developing these qualities? Create a strategy for adding them to your PLN.

3. Make a plan for your social media professional development. What would you like to accomplish? In what months would you like to accomplish these goals?

4. Write down your goals for your career. Do they match what is needed in the current market of professionals? How can you adapt your goals to meet the needs of the current market?

REFERENCES

Bregman, A., Goetzman, G., Hanks, T., Ponsoldt, J., & Ponsoldt, J. (2017). *The Circle* [*Motion Picture*]. United States: STXfilms.

Heid, M. (2018). You asked: Is social media Making Me Miserable? *Time Magazine*. Retrieved from ⟨http://time.com/collection/guide-to-happiness/4882372/social-media-facebook-instagram-unhappy/⟩ (accessed 18.01.21).

Ito, M. (2010). *Hanging out, messing around, and geeking out: Kids living and learning with new media*. Cambridge, MA: MIT Press.

Khedher, M. (2014). Personal branding phenomenon. *International Journal of Information, Business and Management*, *6*(2), 29–40.

Kouzes, J. M., & Posner, B. Z. (2007). *The leadership challenge*. San Francisco, CA: John Wiley & Sons.

Lankau, M. J., & Scandura, T. A. (2002). An investigation of personal learning in mentoring relationships: Content, antecedents, and consequences. *Academy of Management Journal*, *45*(4), 779–790.

Llopis, G. (April 8, 2013). Personal branding is a leadership requirement, not a self-promotion campaign. *Forbes*. Retrieved from ⟨https://www.forbes.com/sites/glennllopis/2013/04/08/personal-branding-is-a-leadership-requirement-not-a-self-promotion-campaign/#2e9be099226f⟩ (accessed 18.01.21).

Peters, T. (August 31, 1997). The brand called you. *Fast Company*. Retrieved from ⟨https://www.fastcompany.com/28905/brand-called-you⟩ (accessed 18.01.21).

Quast, L. (April 22, 2013). Personal branding 101. *Forbes*. Retrieved from ⟨https://www.forbes.com/sites/lisaquast/2013/04/22/personal-branding-101/#74720803297c⟩ (accessed 18.01.21).

Russ, K. R. (2015). Building professional social capital among minority business students. *Academy of Educational Leadership Journal*, *19*(3), 271–279.

Sie, R. L. L., Pataraia, N., Boursinou, E., Rajagopal, K., Margaryan, A., Falconer, I., ... Sloep, P. B. (2013). Goals, motivation for, and outcomes of personal learning through networks: Results of a tweetstorm. *Journal of Educational Technology & Society*, *16*(3), 59–75.

Seibert, S. E., Kraimer, M. L., & Liden, R. C. (2001). A social capital theory of career success. *The Academy of Management Journal, 44*(2), 219–237.

Talan, S. (2017). Is professorial branding for you? Yes, it is. *The Chronicle of Higher Education, 64*(8). Retrieved from ⟨https://www.chronicle.com/article/Is-Professorial-Branding-for/241438⟩ (accessed 18.01.21).

Tour, E. (2017). Teachers' personal learning networks (PLNs): Exploring the nature of self-initiated professional learning online. *Literacy, 51*(1), 11–18.

CHAPTER 4

Social Media Networks for Personal Branding and Career Development

Figure 4.1 Personal branding text concept.

4.1 FACEBOOK

Facebook is the most popular social network in the world. It started as a social network for college students. It has since grown into a resource for connecting with friends, families, businesses, celebrities, and brands. The original incarnation of Facebook was called FacesMash and debuted in October 2003 when Mark Zuckerberg and his classmates collaborated on website design (Mastrioianni, 2016). Facesmash took the form of a game that allowed users to compare pictures of undergraduate students to determine their attractiveness. According to Burns (2017), Facebook made its debut in its current conceptual form in 2004. Initially, the website was restricted to Harvard students. However, access was later offered to university and high school students until it was finally available to the general public.

Facebook is a global phenomenon. As of 2016, 83.6% of its daily active users were based outside North America (Mastrioianni, 2016).

Facebook strives to offer engaging content to users. In fact, it was at the forefront of virtual reality experiences when it first offered 360-degree videos in 2015. It is reported that due to Facebook, the degrees of separation that people experience is 3.5 rather than 6 (Mastrioianni, 2016).

Facebook offers several branding and professional development opportunities. The site features groups of like-minded individuals and posts from popular thought leaders and organizations. Professionals can also establish themselves as a brand by utilizing the posting and page features that are available within Facebook. If you are not a current user of Facebook, take a couple of minutes to browse the site to see what is happening. It is easier to see the content if you set up an account. If you are not ready to get actively involved, you can lurk. You can also limit yourself to "Following" or "Liking" organizational and brand pages. When you do this, no one expects you to share content. You can get started with Facebook using the basic steps provided below. Of course, the website is very comprehensive, and there is more to it than what is presented here. However, this should be sufficient to help you understand how to access and benefit from the basic elements that are offered.

4.1.1 Getting Started With Facebook
4.1.1.1 Signing up for an Account
- Start by going to www.Facebook.com.
- You will be prompted to enter some general information including your first name, last name, mobile phone number or email address, and a password.
- Complete each of the blanks and click on the button to create an account.
- Next, you will need to confirm your account. This step will vary according to whether you have entered an email address or phone number. If you used your mobile phone number, a code will be sent to your phone. If you used an email address, you will need to log into your email to access and follow the directions from Facebook to confirm your account.

4.1.2 Completing Your Profile
Some people skip adding a photo to their Facebook profile. However, you should expect to have one because it is Facebook. A photo will make your profile appear more authentic and personable. You can either take a picture with your webcam or upload one from your computer. If you

don't decide to add a photo in the initial stages, you can always go to your profile page to upload a photo there. Keep in mind that an avatar is fine for your profile picture if you are concerned about other people recognizing you or using your likeness for ill intentions. You can make an avatar by using one of the websites listed below. You can also upload your picture to Microsoft Word and use some of the filters to change it to create an avatar.

- Avachara: https://avachara.com/avatar/
- Avatar Maker: http://avatarmaker.com/
- Cartoonify: https://www.cartoonify.de/
- My Blue Robot: https://mybluerobot.com/create-your-own-avatar/

4.1.3 The About Page

Use the About page to tell everyone who you are. It is advisable that you are careful about the amount of information you share on this page. The page will have input fields through which you provide basic information about how people can contact you, where you live, where you went to college, your high school, hometown, and the things you are interested in. Click on the plus sign next to each heading and enter your information.

If you are trying to be professional, you probably don't want to tell your future or current employer that you are interested in sharing photos of the parts of your body that have piercings. If your interest is something that you would not like to talk about at work, don't publish it on a public Facebook page.

While Facebook does have a form for contact information on the About page, it is optional, and you don't need to provide contact details to access the website. People can be malicious and will use Facebook to gather information about your life. Do you really want to add your personal address or mobile phone number? Don't post information that a criminal or someone who does not like you can use against you.

Adding your website and other social media links will support your personal branding efforts and help you to establish a public face across multiple networks. After you complete the forms, be sure to save your changes. Note that you can decide how the information in each section is shared. You have the option to use custom settings. Custom settings allow you to specify who you would and would not like to share information with. People who are on the "Don't share with" list are not notified about the status you have assigned to them.

4.1.4 How Facebook Pages Are Set Up

Some basic information is displayed on each Facebook page. The left side of the page serves as a navigation bar. It will include a link to go to your profile, see your News Feed, and use the Messenger. Below these links, you can explore the following: Groups, Pages, Events, Friend lists, On This Day, Games, and more.

The middle of the page displays your News Feed. At the top of the page, you will find a text box for creating messages. Below the textbox, you can see videos, photos, and posts that were published by friends and entities that you follow.

The final column on the right has information from Facebook. At the top of the column, you can see what's trending on Facebook. Trends are divided by top trends, politics, science and technology, sports, and entertainment. Other areas in the third column may include suggestions for people who are potential friends, sponsored ads, and a small section to select the language that you would like to read.

There is a search box at the top of the page. It provides links to your profile, Home, Find Friends, Friend Requests, Messages, Notifications, and Help. The drop-down menu next to Help will let you perform various activities such as creating your own page, creating ads, finding groups, creating fundraisers, and logging out.

4.1.5 Writing a Facebook Post

One of the simplest things you can do on Facebook is write a single post. Creating a post only takes a few minutes. Consider writing your posts and spell checking them in Word before publishing them.

- After you have written your post, go to Facebook.com and sign in to get started.
- Once you are on your profile, choose the Make Post option.
- Paste or write in your post. Remember that you can easily add links to the post simply by pasting the link after you write the post. Usually, this will create an automatic link to the site that you want to share. Including a link will provide a thumbnail based on the website.
- Decide if you want to add other elements to your post such as photos and videos, emojis to indicate your feelings, a check in for a recent location, a poll, or a tag for a friend. You can decide not to add anything but text.

- Once you are ready to post, choose who can see the post. Options include limiting the post to yourself, your friends, or making it public. Usually, posts are automatically set to public.
- When you are done, click on the Post button to share your thoughts (Box 4.1).

4.1.6 Commenting on a Facebook Post

There will probably come a time when you want to comment on a post that was published by someone else. It is easy to leave a comment. Ideally, you want to evaluate the situation before you do so. Who are you interacting with? What type of people follow them? Will your comment incite controversy? Write down your comment and proofread it.

- Navigate to the post that you want to respond to.
- Press the Comment button.
- Paste or write your comment directly under that post. You can add images, GIFs, stickers, or a reaction.
- Press the Enter key on your keyboard to publish your comment.
- Sometimes your comments will get responses. If you want to reply to these comments, press the Reply button under the desired comment.

BOX 4.1 What kind of social media posts get the most likes?

kYmberly Keeton—For me, typically, the most likes come from library nostalgia, personal rants, and my writing. I also think that my photos also take people places they cannot go, so they actually go to conferences with me, and travel to places with me.

Dr. Spencer Keralis—The funny posts and stupid memes get the most likes. I could post the best article ever on whatever it is I'm working on right now and, five people will like it. I could post a cat meme, or I could post an Instagram picture of my cat, doing something ridiculous. That will get 50 likes from people who are way above my pay grade in my field. But likes aren't necessarily a measure of impact.

I think getting likes for a cat meme is just as legitimate as getting likes when you post your scholarly work because it's helping you build that network. So, thinking about likes as impact isn't necessarily the best way to do it. Neither is retweets because people will retweet cat memes more than they'll retweet scholarly articles.

I do get a lot of likes or retweets when we post events. Whether it's my conference that I organize or speakers that we bring in or other events.

Note that in addition to commenting on posts, you can just Like them or Share them.

4.1.7 The Friends Page

What would Facebook be without friends? As indicated by the name of the page, the Friends page displays your friends and helps you to find more friends. In Facebook, a friend is a person who has joined your social network. You are connected to them. On Facebook, a friend may not be someone who you are close to. They could be someone who requested to be part of your network after reading something that you wrote. Conversely, they could be a family member whom you have known since birth.

One can search for friends to add. Click on the Find Friends button. On the Friends page, there will be a button under the Friends tab. There is another link at the top of the Facebook page.

Follow these directions to find a friend:

- Click on the Find Friends button. If you have friend requests, you will see a list of them. Below the list of friends, you will see Facebook's list of People You May Know. This list originates from your location and information that you have added while setting up your Facebook profile. The page will populate with more suggestions as you scroll down.
- When you find someone who you would like to connect with, click on the Add Friend button. Alternatively, if you know that there is someone who you do not want to connect with and would like removed from your list, click on the Remove button.
- The suggestions made by Facebook may not be suitable for you. In this case, look at the right side of the page to view more options for finding and adding friends .
- You can upload your contact list.
- You can search for friends. You can search by name, school, and location. As you type your information into the fields, Facebook will try to make suggestions that are relevant to you. If none of the selections work, finish typing in your search term. You can search using multiple search criteria. For example, you can search for Jane Doe in the Bronx, New York.
- The results will appear on the left under People You Know. When you find someone that matches your criteria, click on the Add Friend button.

- Should your search using the filters fail to return results, you still have another option to find a long lost friend. Simply use the search box at the top of the page.

When you invite a person to join your network as a friend, they are not automatically added to your list of friends. They are sent an invitation that they must accept to officially become a friend. There is a chance that your request to connect will be rejected or just sit until the person decides to accept or decline it. If they accept, you will see them in your friend list. If they accept, you will see them in your friend list. If not, you will not receive notification. You can assume that the person did not want to be your friend.

4.1.8 Reviewing Friend Requests

Facebook is a social network, and you are bound to get a request from someone to be a friend. You can decide whether you want to accept or decline requests. The icon at the top of the Facebook page that features two silhouettes is for friend requests.

- Click the icon to review your friend requests.
- When the page loads, click the Confirm button to accept the person as a friend. Click on Delete Request to decline their offer. You can just let it sit too.

4.1.9 Saying Goodbye to a Friend

I am not literally telling you to say goodbye verbally to someone. Instead, it is important for you to know that you are not required to keep a person as a friend on Facebook. Perhaps they have been publishing posts that you find counterproductive to your career. Maybe the person publishes too many posts. Perhaps you have decided that you do not want your coworkers to be able to see your information on Facebook anymore. In these cases, it is time to unfriend people. Don't worry. Any person who you unfriend will not receive a notification telling them that you have disowned them. Use this process to unfriend a person:

- Click on your name at the top of the page to go to your Timeline.
- Click on the Friends page in the menu at the top of the page.
- Find the person with whom you no longer want to be friends.
- Click on the Friend button to unfriend them.

4.1.10 Entity Pages on Facebook

There are many companies, celebrities, organizations, businesses, and brands on Facebook. For the purposes of brevity, in this section, all of them will be referred to as *entities*. The homepage of an entity will share a lot of information about it. You will be able to review details that they have shared such as if they are a nonprofit organization. Facebook also displays the organization's star rating feedback. If the entity has completed its profile, you will see its location, phone number, the time it takes for the entity to reply to messages, and its email address. Details about the community surrounding the organization will include how many people follow, like, and have sent a message to the organization within the past month.

Beneath the About section, you will see other pages that have liked the organization's page. This is helpful when you are looking for similar entities to follow. Examine the list to determine if there are any entities that can meet your needs, in conjunction with the organization that you are already interested in.

4.1.11 Following an Entity

- Search for the entity using the search tool.
- If your entity appears at the top, you can select it right away. You can also click to see all the results.
- When the page loads, you will see a section for Pages and another for Public Posts.
- You can always browse the posts, but for now, let's look at the Pages.
- Click on the Page that you are interested in.
- Once on the home page of an entity, you can review the links that describe the organization. These page links may include About, Photos, Events, and Videos.
- When the page loads, click on the Follow button. The button will change to Following. If you change your mind about following the organization, click on the Following button and you can unfollow the organization from there.
- When you **Like** a page on Facebook, it means that you will be following it too. When you post something, the entity will see what you post. If you follow a page, it does not mean that you like it. However, you will see the posts it publishes.

4.1.12 Finding Facebook Groups

Facebook has thousands of groups to choose from. If you want to enjoy Facebook's groups feature, you can follow a few simple steps to connect. Keep in mind the fact that some groups are not advertised. There are open groups that are viewable when you browse the group and can be found through search engines. Then there are closed groups. In a closed group, the group administrator must approve new members. The names of the members, the group description, and the group name can still be seen online. Only group members can view the posts published by these groups. Then there are secret groups that cannot be viewed by the public. You must be invited by a member to join a secret group. Use the steps outlined below to join a public or closed group.

4.1.12.1 Option 1
• First, enter your Facebook profile and then select Explore/Groups on the left side of your screen.
• Once you are in the Groups section, you can manage your own groups or discover new ones.
• Press the Discover button, and you will see groups that you can join. Depending on your browsing history, Facebook will show groups that you may be interested in. For instance, there will be local and recommended groups. There is also an option to create your own group.

4.1.12.2 Option 2
• Navigate to your home page.
• Click in the search box and enter a search term.
• When the page loads, look for the Groups link at the top of the page and click on the link.
• Scroll down the page to find groups that you like.
• There are options to filter groups. For example, you can look at any group that Facebook has related to your terms. You can look at public and closed groups. There is also an option to look at groups that your friends are members of.

4.1.13 Joining a Facebook Group

Note that you can review the descriptions of the groups, the number of members, and the number of posts per day that the group publishes. If you are sure that you want to be a member of a group when it shows in the search results, you can go ahead and click on the + Join button on the page.

Alternatively, you can click on the group name to learn more about it. You can see who the administrator of the group is. You can browse the list of group members too. There are a few indicators that you should consider when you are joining a group.

- Do the members seem as if they are professional?
- Are the posts professional?
- Is the group worth joining? If there is nothing going on, why waste your time?
- Is the location of the group relevant to your needs? For example, would you join a job search group that only publishes posts for jobs in Australia if you have no intention of moving there to get a job?
- Does the group represent an established organization or is it run by a credible person?
- Do you want to be associated with the topic of the group professionally? Would the topic of the group hurt your career?
- Are some of the members of the group people that you do not wish to associate with?
- If the group is suitable, click on the + Join Group on the group's profile page.

4.2 LINKEDIN

Consider LinkedIn to be the premier social networking website for making professional connections. LinkedIn helps users to create a social media presence that centers around their work experience and skills. It was created to help professionals to connect with similar specialists, seek job opportunities, recruit viable candidates, and promote businesses.

LinkedIn is great for beginning library and information science (LIS) professionals, those looking for new jobs, and for those who want to engage in entrepreneurial endeavors. LinkedIn can be a great source for learning about what people have to say about the latest trends. You can also connect with people with similar interests. LinkedIn is suitable for viewing the profiles of people that you admire. Read about their experience and the skills that other people endorse them as having.

Looking at the skills that other people have listed will help you to decide how to market your own skills on LinkedIn. The primary audience for LinkedIn is educated professionals. Depending on the way you use LinkedIn, you can increase your visibility by writing visible content and enhancing your portfolio. LinkedIn will allow you to build your professional learning network while connecting with past colleagues, friends, and acquaintances. LinkedIn is also a way to celebrate the accomplishments of people who are in your contact list. Congratulate them on events such as birthdays and work anniversaries.

4.2.1 Setting Up a LinkedIn Profile

Start by going to LinkedIn to sign up. Use this link https://linkedin.com/reg/join. Setting up a LinkedIn profile is quick and easy. However, it is also important to manage how you are viewed. People who have never previously met you may form a judgment on you based on the information you share on your LinkedIn profile. Follow the prompts that LinkedIn gives you to set up your account. You may be prompted to share the following information:

- A password. LinkedIn allows networkers to sign up using their Google and Facebook accounts.
- Your job information
- Your location
- Imported email contacts if desired
- A valid email address
- Your selection of the free or paid subscription

After you enter the necessary information, you will need to complete additional elements of your profile. Input a professional photo. The headline for your profile comes from the position that you enter on your profile. It can be edited. Some people choose to enter their mission statements as their headlines (LinkedIn, 2015). The headline is directly below your name. Gather your information about your education. You can add each of your degrees and certificates. LinkedIn will suggest skills based on your profile, and you can add more.

Finally, develop your summary. The summary is where you can define your professional brand. The summary should include your interests, career aspirations, and what makes you unique. List the specialties that make you marketable. Describe your niche. Let people know what your goals are. You might consider including an invitation to contact you for professional inquiries. Videos, articles, and slideshows can be used to enhance your profile. Use simple English that a layman can understand. LinkedIn recommends avoiding the words listed in Fig. 4.2 because they

Figure 4.2 Words that are overused in LinkedIn profiles.

Table 4.1 Access to LinkedIn features for company pages

Freemium	Premium customers
News, announcements, and product updates	Employee statistics
Individuals that are connected to the company	Employee length of employment
Company showcase pages	Distribution of employees by position
Links to affiliated and related companies	Job openings by position
Job listings	See jobs opportunities where you would have an advantage

are overused (LinkedIn, 2015, para. 10). When you are done, consider asking a colleague to proofread the summary for you. LinkedIn will automatically judge the strength of your profile. Use the tips offered to make improvements.

4.2.2 Learning About Companies

LinkedIn is not just for individuals. Companies use LinkedIn to publish news and profiles. Some companies post their job opportunities on LinkedIn. An organization's page on LinkedIn will give you basic information about the firm such as the company's website, size, and business sector. If you follow a company, you can see their information on your LinkedIn homepage feed. LinkedIn (2016) notes that there are differences between what free and premium users can view on the network (see Table 4.1). Reviewing the profile of a company on LinkedIn is a good way to perform some preliminary research before job interviews. The information is consolidated and will provide a foundation for the questions that you can ask during an interview. Moreover, you will want to be knowledgeable about the organization and its employees just in case you get asked a question about the organization. Brush up with intel and be prepared to dazzle the recruiter or search committee.

4.2.3 LinkedIn Groups

LinkedIn is not just a fan club. It is also a place to converse with like-minded professionals. The reputation that you create as a professional is important. You can join an established LinkedIn group or start your own. By participating in groups, you are developing an audience for free. As you communicate new ideas, people will begin to trust your brand and understand what you offer as a professional. Here are some things that you can use a group for.

- To discuss topics with your connections and audience.
- To encourage people to visit your websites and social media pages.
- To promote yourself as an expert and leader.
- To help other people who have questions about things that you have experience with.
- To increase your connections on LinkedIn and other social networking sites.
- To attract the attention of potential employers.

Keep in mind that the groups that you join also tell people about who you are. Join groups that represent that image that you want to create. If you are a librarian and you join 20 groups on farming and post articles about farming instead of focusing on librarianship, it is not likely that the people on LinkedIn will think of you as a librarian. They will think of you as a farmer. Focus on your branding. If you join groups relevant to your interests, you will be able to connect with other people who have the potential to help you improve your career. When you are considering joining a group, there are some additional questions you should ask:

- Where is the group located? Is it just for a specific region? If you have a specific group you need to reach based on geography, you will need to consider the location.
- What types of people are in the group?
- How much experience do the group members have?
- Are the group members in advanced positions?
- What are the roles of the group members within their organization?

- Does the group have members who appear to have an active stream of communication?
- Who are the administrators of the group? Do they have strong reputations?

Certainly, anyone that you interact with in a group could be a potential recruiter in the future. However, you want to tailor your conversation according to who you are interacting with. As you interact with the group, provide frequent updates with a stream of information that the group will find helpful. This information can be posted as articles on your LinkedIn page. Write a variety of positive stories or tips related to your skills. You will also want to look within the group for topics that can be helpful. As you build your content, you can begin to create a brand that people can trust.

If you are seeking speaking engagements, posting content and interacting with other professionals can be beneficial. People will begin to browse your content and decide if they want to communicate with you based on the content. Do not be surprised if you begin to get speaking and writing opportunities based on the information that you have posted on LinkedIn and other networks.

4.2.4 How to Find a Group

People form groups for many reasons. These reasons include professional interests, hobbies, job messages, and alumni networking. LinkedIn defines its groups as Standard or Unlisted. The groups that a person is a member of will show on the Highlights section of their profile. Standard groups can be found by searching LinkedIn and search engines. One must be a member of LinkedIn to join these groups. If you are not a member of a group, you will not be able to see the conversations that take place in the group. One cannot search for an Unlisted Group; they can be accessed by invitation only. These groups are also not visible to other people on your profile page. You can also manage how your membership of groups is displayed on your profile page. If you belong to a controversial group, a group that you do not want other people to know about, or are looking for a job, it is wise to edit your settings. There are a couple of ways to find a group to join.

4.2.4.1 First Option: By Invitation

LinkedIn has unlisted groups. The only way you can join these groups is to be invited. These groups cannot be found by using a search engine or the LinkedIn search functionality. The administrators have set them up so that they are private. If you have heard of a group, feel you fit the criteria, and know someone who is in it, ask for an invitation. When you receive the invitation, click on the link to join the group.

4.2.4.2 Second Option: By Searching

- You can start at https://www.linkedin.com/feed/ and click in the search box.
- If you know the name of the group you want to join, type the name in the search box.
- If you do not know the name of the group, type in a keyword.
- Leave the cursor in the box, and you will notice that your search results are divided into various categories that include companies, your connections, groups, schools, and showcase pages. You will also see an option to see all the results associated with your search term at the bottom of the results box.
- When the page loads, you will be provided with several options that you can use to narrow down the results. You can select people, jobs, and content. There is also a more button with a drop-down arrow. Click the arrow, and you will find options to select companies, groups, and school. You can also filter by locations, your connections, and current companies.
- Use the drop-down menu next to More to select Groups. When the page loads, look through the groups and select the groups that fit your needs. Don't forget that you can filter the results.

4.2.4.3 Third Option: By Browsing

- You can start at https://www.linkedin.com/feed/ and click on the Work icon at the top of the page.
- Select Groups from the drop-down menu.
- When the page loads, click on the Discover tab at the top of the page. LinkedIn will share group recommendations with you. Scroll down the page to browse the suggestions.
- When you find a group that you like, you could go ahead and click on the link to "Ask to Join" the group. Alternatively, you could click on the link to access more information about it.
- If you click on the link to read about the group, the About page will provide a summary of who manages the group and your connections within the group.
- If the group meets your needs, use the "Ask to Join" link at the top of the page.

4.2.5 Setting Up Your Own Group

One way to personalize and build a personal learning network (PLN) is to create a LinkedIn group around your interests. Any member of LinkedIn can create a group. Follow these steps to create your own.

- You can begin by either clicking on the Groups icon at the top of your page or by clicking on the Work icon and using the drop-down menu to access groups.
- When the group page loads, click on My Groups.
- You will see a Create Group button on the page.
- There will be several text boxes to complete.
- Start by giving your group a title.
- Next, if you have a logo, upload it. You can create a logo in a program such as Canva (https://www.canva.com/) or PicMonkey (https://www.picmonkey.com). In addition, VistaPrint (https://www.vistaprint.com) is a paid service that will allow you to create your own logo or have one designed for you.
- Type in a description of the group.
- Type the group rules. This is optional but highly advisable if you wish to eliminate miscommunication.
- Decide if your group will be a Standard group or an Unlisted group.

4.2.6 Establishing Group Rules

Developing rules for your PLN will help you to manage it. Plenty of people may decide to join your group. You cannot assume that everyone will behave the same way that you do. You want to be able to clearly indicate your requirements for being part of your PLN. After all, you are responsible for the group, and the activities within it can either positively or negatively impact your reputation. When you write your group rules, consider adding these elements:

- Share why the group is necessary and the purpose it will fulfill for those who join.
- Describe the membership criteria. Can anyone join your group regardless of who they are? Or, do you have specific goals about what you want to accomplish? Who can help you accomplish your goals? Will your group be a personal learning network (PLN)? If so, you want to invite experts or people that are willing to work towards becoming experts to share information. Carefully defining your group

will allow you to provide information and receive information from people that understand your needs.

- Explain the type of information that people can post in your group. Are they allowed to post jobs? Are they allowed to post jobs? If so, will the job posts be limited to the jobs section of the group? Can people post advertisements for their businesses and is self-promotion okay?
- Explain the type of dialogue that is expected. Do you promote casual conservations, or do you want them to be professional? Are people allowed to use profanity?
- Finally, what will be the consequences of not adhering to the rules? Will people receive a warning? Or will they immediately be eliminated from the group?

4.2.7 Things to Remember About Groups

Here are some things that you need to know about LinkedIn Groups.
- The groups that you belong to are displayed on your LinkedIn page.
- People can find you by looking in a group.
- Groups have rules that you should read before posting
- Any LinkedIn member can start a LinkedIn group.
- Some groups include job posts that are targeted at members of specific groups.
- You can be invited to join groups that are unlisted.
- You can only have 10 requests to join active groups at any one time.
- You can start 30 groups.
- You can be a member of 100 groups.
- Groups are limited to 20,000 members.
- Just 1 person can own a group.
- 10 people can be given administrative privileges for a group that you create.

4.2.8 Types of LinkedIn Connections

LinkedIn has several types of connections for members of the network. A first degree connection is someone who is in your network because you contacted them, and they accepted your invitation, or they contacted you and you accepted their invitation. If you click on the connections in your profile, you can send these people a message via LinkedIn. It follows that a person is a second degree connection if they are connected to one of your first degree connections. If you want them to become a first degree connection, click on the Connect button on their profile or in the People You May Know of your own My Network page. A third degree connection is someone who is connected to someone who is your second degree connection. The more first degree connections you have, the more you will be visible to other people on LinkedIn. Likewise, you will be able to see more profiles for your second and third degree connections. Connections are helpful because, despite the ability to search for profiles, LinkedIn is a large network. Unless you personally know someone to search for their name, you may not find them on LinkedIn.

Remember that it is easy to simply click on the Connect button. However, many LinkedIn members like to receive an invitation with a personal note. To send a personal note with an invitation:

- Go the member's profile.
- Click on the Connect button.
- You will see a pop-up window that will allow you to send a note with the invitation.
- Click on the Add A Note button.
- Write the message to include in the invitation.
- Click the Send Now button.

4.2.9 Searching for People on LinkedIn

If your invitation is accepted, you will see a note on your Notifications page and/or you will receive an email with the update.

- You can use the search box at the top of the page to find new people to connect with. Follow these directions.
  - Click on the search box.
  - If you have a name in mind, enter the name.
  - If you do not have a name, look at the drop-down menu that opens when you click in the search box.
  - Click on People to search for people.
  - A page will load with a list of people. This list will begin with your second degree connections.

4.3 TWITTER

As I write this, I think back to the Spring semester of 2009, when I was sitting in a doctoral course that I wasn't excited about taking. My instructor was talking about how great she thought Twitter was. I sat thinking to myself, "Why is this included in our lecture? Can you talk about something that is related to my future? What can I accomplish with 140 characters anyway?" I was quite close to verbalizing my annoyance with "That's stupid!" when we moved on (Box 4.2).

Yet, here I am today telling you that Twitter is not stupid at all. I admit that I was late to the Twitter party. I have a couple of anonymous accounts. I use it mainly for research and for looking at trends. I can't say that I am the most active person on Twitter. But what I can say is that it is a valuable resource. Twitter has come a long way with its 140 characters. Ironically, in its first iteration, Twitter did not limit the number of characters. This began when the company went public (Picard, 2017). Among its many uses, it is a professional development tool, a way to reach loved ones and friends, a tool for activism, a facilitator for community outreach, and even an influencer of politics. Some people think of Twitter as an instant newsletter because breaking news is frequently shared on Twitter (Picard, 2017). Twitter users capitalize on its reach to influence politics, promote and criticize products, and educate others about issues.

Twitter is a microblogging platform that began in 2006 (Van Dijck, 2013). EMarketer estimated that in 2017, Twitter had 255.3 million users worldwide. It was listed as the sixth most used social networking site in the United States in 2017 (Statista, 2018b).

Globally, Twitter is listed as the 11th most popular social network online with 330 million users (Statista, 2018a). It has become so important that it has been engrained in politics. World leaders can be found using Twitter to reach the masses. As of May 2017, the world leaders with the most popular accounts on Twitter (with followers in the millions) were Pope Francis (33.72), Donald Trump (30.13), Narendra Modi (30.06), and the Prime Minister of India (18.04) (Twiplomacy, 2017).

Many people like Twitter because it breaks down the barriers of communication. In the past, a regular person may have never been noticed by

BOX 4.2 Why do you use Twitter professionally?

Ayla Stein—Any other social media platform is not as current as Twitter. In my view, Twitter is the most current with what people are talking about. It has news and pop culture, but also has a lot of librarianship news as well. Twitter is where I learn about a lot of new projects that I need to look into.

the President of the United States. But today, Donald Trump is an avid Tweeter who exchanges comments with the average person via the Twitter platform. Engaging in conversation with high-profile people was not this easy in the past (Box 4.3).

Most Twitter profiles are public, allowing anyone to follow a person who they normally would not be able to communicate with. You can follow anyone who you want to follow and vice versa. Unlike LinkedIn for example, a person does not have to accept your request to follow them. This means that you can see anything that they post if their account is public. If someone begins to get pushy on Twitter, you can block them from following you.

But access to high-profile people is not the only thing that makes Twitter an interesting platform. Twitter fosters a global community where news is available immediately. I recall watching the breaking news about a shooting that occurred in Dallas, Texas, during a peaceful demonstration against police shootings. The event was considered to be the deadliest attack against law enforcement in the United States since the 9/11 attacks (NBC 5 Staff, 2016). While CNN, MSNBC, and FOX News struggled to keep up with the latest news, updates on Twitter provided the perspectives of the individuals who were experiencing the events firsthand. The police department Tweeted updates as well. Some news outlets began reporting the information that was shared on social media so that they could share the details quicker.

Similarly, Twitter was used heavily by the public in the aftermath of the Boston Bombing (Schultz, 2013). However, just 20% of what was posted revealed the truth about the event. Half of the Tweets contained opinions, and 29% were based on fake content. Unfortunately, the fake content that is posted on Twitter can be passed along by well-meaning

BOX 4.3 How does social media help with networking?

Greg Hardin—There have been examples where I have reached out to people that I would not have reached out to otherwise. They were people in higher positions, or authorities in certain areas. If you see that they are very active on social media, and you're able to send a very short, private message, or a message. I think that's much more casual than sending them an email. If they're very active on social media, they are putting themselves out there and are usually open to those kinds of interactions, or not threatened by them.

individuals who do not take the time to verify the facts. Hence, rumors posted on social media can have dire consequences. For example, several stories were posted on social media that implicated presidential candidate Hillary Clinton in a child-sex trafficking ring located inside the Comet Ping Pong pizzeria. The story (referred to as Pizzagate) was proven to be wrong (Kessler, 2016), but not before Edgar Maddison Welch went to the restaurant in December 2016 and fired a gun (Siddiqui & Svrluga, 2016). To make a long story short, one must take the information that is shared on Twitter and other social media networks with a pinch of salt.

4.3.1 Getting Started with Twitter

Twitter has apps for Android, IOS (Apple), and Windows devices. The steps outlined below focus on using Twitter from a desktop computer. Follow the prompts from Twitter.

- Begin by entering an email address or phone number.
- Then enter a password.
- Click on the Get Started button.
- Type in your full name. In some cases, you may want to use your brand if you have a pseudonym.

You can choose to let Twitter personalize your content. I don't select this option because I would not like Twitter finding content related to my hobbies when I use it for research and professional development purposes. This option allows Twitter to track the websites that you visit to customize the ads and content in your timeline (Twitter, 2018b). If you check this box when you sign up, you can always turn this feature off after observing how it works. Just go to your profile and adjust your settings.

Note that the advanced options for Twitter will let people find you using your email address or phone number. Adjust these settings according to your preferences. Go to the next step to enter your phone number.

4.3.2 The Twitter Home Page

Let's look at the basics of what is on a Twitter home page. Each Twitter page displays the person or organization name under a profile picture. Again, the profile will have a check mark displayed in the middle of a blue circle next to the name if it is verified. Under the name, you will see the Twitter handle. A Twitter handle will start with an "@" sign. It is the person or organization's username.

A Twitter handle is one way to show your brand. It can consist of a combination of letters, numbers, and characters. If you are having trouble choosing a name, Twitter will give you some ideas. But be selective about the name that you opt for. Twitter will let you change your handle, but if you are establishing an account and making connections, you don't want to keep changing your identity. When I tried to claim my name on Twitter, I found that it was already taken. Many people start their handles with "The Real" or "I Am." Eventually, I used a combination of my initials, last name, and job title for my professional profile. In any case, the handle needs to be one that carries through your other social media identities. Try to use the same handle for all of them. Here are some quick tips for choosing a handle:

- Do some research to ensure that the handle that you are choosing is not too similar to another handle.
- If your name is not available, choose a handle that represents your brand. If you are interested in branding yourself as a librarian who is interested in technology trends, your handle might be @knowtechlib.
- Try to keep your username short.
- Unless you are looking for controversy, create a neutral username. For example, @icantstandlibraries would not be a good way to make connections with librarians.

Next, Twitter will populate information that further identifies the organization or person. The description of the organization is under the handle. The location appears next. If a website is listed, the link will be displayed. The profile will also display the date that the individual or organization joined Twitter. Two blue buttons are under the date. They will allow you to Tweet to or send a message to the person or organization. If you have a Twitter account and are signed in, you can see how many people or organizations follow the person or organization that you are viewing. This is a good way to find additional people to follow with common interests.

At the top of the page, you can see how many Tweets have been sent from the account. A Tweet is a short 140-character message sent from Twitter. Next to the number of Tweets, you will see who the account is following and the account's followers; a follower or organization that has chosen to see the Tweets issued by that account. When they log into their account, your Tweets will show in their Twitter feed. You can see who you are following or who is following you by clicking on the Following or Followers link. The number of Likes is displayed next to the

Followers. When someone Likes a Tweet or a Moment, it means that they agree with and/or appreciate the content of the Tweet. They are supporting the message.

Twitter also has Lists. Lists are compilations of Twitter users that have specific characteristics. Several accounts can be placed on a list that revolves around a topic of choice. When a list is viewed, the Tweets that are viewed will be limited to the accounts that are on that list. You can subscribe to lists created by others and create your own. Besides being able to categorize people, another benefit of a Twitter list is that you can follow people without officially following them and adding them to your feed.

The Media link contains the media timeline or a list of photos, videos, and GIFs that have been uploaded to an account. The media tab will display the content that has been uploaded in chronological order.

Navigate to your home page after you have logged in by clicking on the birdhouse icon that is displayed at the top of the page. Your homepage will include the feed from accounts that you follow. On the left side of your page, Twitter will make suggestions about who you should follow and show trends that you may be interested in. Twitter automatically populates trends that are based on who you are currently following and your location. You can also find your trends on your Notifications and search results. Notifications on Twitter tell you how people are reacting to your Tweets. If you click on Notifications, you can view who has mentioned you, liked, and retweeted your Tweets.

Messages will show you the private messages you have received from other people on Twitter. To send a message, click on the Messages link and enter a name. Next, follow the prompts and write the message.

The Moments icon is a lightning bolt. A Moment is a set of Tweets that have been gathered into a story in a slideshow format. While you may not have set up moments, you can still view Moments that have been compiled by Twitter for you. If videos are embedded in the Moment that you are viewing, they will automatically play as you scroll down the page. A Moment can include Tweets and media that have been curated by a user. Moments are displayed by Twitter in categories that include Today, News, Sports, Entertainment, and Fun.

4.3.3 Reading Tweets

You can read Tweets by accessing your Twitter Feed on your homepage. Click on the birdcage. This serves as the home icon through which you can return to your home page at any time. You will see that the newest Tweets are listed first. Your Tweets will be mixed in with the Tweets from people and organizations that you follow. Twitter includes promoted Tweets from advertisers.

4.3.4 Posting Your Own Tweet

- No matter where you are on Twitter, when you are logged in, you can send a Tweet. A Tweet button appears at the top of the screen in the toolbar on every page.
- Follow these directions to send a Tweet:
  - Find and click on the Tweet button in the toolbar.
  - Click on the Tweet button.
  - A pop-up box will display.
  - Type in your message. You can mention other people and organizations. A mention is when you write about an organization or person in your Tweet. When people mention you by your user handle, it will show in your Twitter feed. A mention is a great way to get someone to notice you and to start a conversation. If you don't know the username of the individual or organization that you want to refer to, try looking it up by using the Twitter search functionality at the top of the page. Another alternative would be to open the Tweet box. Next, type in the ampersand (@) followed by the beginning of the username. Twitter will make several suggestions of usernames to complete what you have begun typing.

Remember, when you start a message with a handle (@username), the message will only go to people the user and the followers that you and the user have in common. Put the handle at the end of the Tweet or put a period in front of it to send the message to a broader audience.

For example, writing @alaannual would just send the Tweet to Alaannual and the followers you have in common.

- @alaannual Great session on makerspaces #alaannual

Using one of these options would send the Tweet to everyone on Twitter who is interested in @alaannual.

- .@alaannual Great session on makerspaces #alaannual
- Great session on makerspaces! .@alaannual #alaannual

You can include more than text in Tweets. There are several options at the bottom of the box when you compose a message. You can include videos and pictures, an animated GIF, a poll, and links. The GIFs are meant to be humorous and are provided by Twitter. They are broken down into various categories such as Agree, High Five, and Thumbs Down. It is easy to put a link in your Tweet. Type it in or copy and paste it in from your browser. A URL shortener can come in handy to preserve the 140-character limit. Examples of websites that shorten URLs include

- bit.ly—https://bitly.com/
- Google URL Shortener—https://goo.gl/
- IS Gd—https://is.gd/

4.3.5 Interacting with Tweets

There are a couple of ways that you can interact with Tweets. If you like a Tweet, click on the heart to let people know that you like it, the heart will fill in indicating that you liked the Tweet. If you click on the square with the arrows, you can retweet a Tweet. A retweet is a way of sharing what someone else has said. Retweeting can be good when something comes up that you are passionate about or that you think is worthwhile mentioning. Try to make a statement when you retweet a message. Otherwise, your audience is not getting your authentic message. When you add a statement before you send a retweet, the Tweet is known as a Quote Tweet.

4.3.5.1 Follow These Steps to Retweet

Find the message that you want to retweet in your Twitter feed.
- Click on the message.
- Click the box with the two arrows.
- Click on the Retweet button.

4.3.5.2 Follow These Steps to Publish a Quote Tweet

Find that message that you want to retweet in your Twitter feed.
- Click on the message.
- Click the box with the two arrows.
- Type a message.
- Click on the Retweet button.

You can reply to a Tweet. A reply will send a response to a Tweet directly to the person or organization that issued the original Tweet. The great thing about this is that you can reply to anyone (if they have not blocked you). For example, if you want to reply to your congressman or the president, you can do so at any time. Although you may never be able to talk with them face-to-face, you can sit on your couch in your pajamas and interact with them tonight at any time.

There is a comment icon. By clicking on this, you can publish a public comment about a Tweet that other people can see. Comments are a way to engage in a conversation with the originator of a Tweet. If the conversation is interesting enough, several people will post direct comments that respond to what you have posted. Finally, you can send a private message about a Tweet by clicking on the Envelope icon.

All Tweets do not have hashtags. When a Tweet has a hashtag, you can click on it and see what the most recent conferences regarding the hashtag are about. People will frequently post URLs in Tweets. Clicking on them will take you to the content. You are advised to be careful about the URLs that you click on. Consider the extent to which you perceive the person who posted the URL to be trustworthy. Otherwise, you may find yourself with a virus on your computer from using social media. While you can never completely trust the authenticity of social media and there is a risk that accounts can be hacked, you can still use the handle in the picture to view the profile of the person or organization who has Tweeted.

4.3.6 What is a Hashtag?

A hashtag is a way to categorize a Tweet. Think of it as a keyword. When a pound (#) symbol is placed in front of a group of words and or numbers, the Tweets containing the hashtag will be grouped together in Twitter searches. A hashtag can be placed anywhere in the body of a Tweet. Hashtags are a way to have a conversation on Twitter. For example, many people host Twitter chats or simultaneously Tweet during a designated time about a topic on Twitter by using hashtags. Most people use hashtags in their Tweets because the number of people using the same hashtag will help determine if the hashtag topic is current and trending. In fact, your Twitter homepage will display a list of trends for you that includes hashtags. Hashtags within Tweets are links that show other Tweets with the same hashtag. See Appendix 7 for some examples of popular hashtags that are relevant to librarians and their meanings, as described on Hashtags.org.

4.3.7 How to Create a Hashtag

Think of a hashtag as sort of a tagline that people can use to identify a topic. People use hashtags to help other people find information. Note that hashtags are not a creation of the original Twitter developers. They are not owned by one person. As usual, a very creative person was on Twitter and decided to use the first hashtag to make their information searchable. Hashtags work for Twitter, but Twitter does not have an official way for you to subscribe to a hashtag. (If This Then That, Zapier, and HootSuite are good ways to "follow" a hashtag for an extended amount of time.) However, you can subscribe to a person that frequently uses a hashtag that you are interested in. Hashtags also work in other social networks such as Facebook, Google +, and Instagram (Box 4.4).

4.3.8 Adding Multimedia to Tweets

You can add pictures and videos to Tweets.

- A pop-up box will open to compose your Tweet.
- Click on the Picture icon. It is currently a square with triangles that resemble mountain peaks.
- Another box will open that will allow you to select pictures from your computer.
- Select your picture or video and click on Open.
- Twitter will ask you to describe who is in the photo. You can search and tag 10 people or skip this part.
- If you decide to add a video, a box will open that will enable you to trim the video.
- Click the Done button when you are finished trimming your video.
- Review your picture and/or video. An "X" shows in the corner of video and photo thumbnails that will allow you to delete them.

BOX 4.4 How do you increase your social media followers?

Ayla Stein—*I would say my social media followers increase the most during conferences. When you Tweet on the conference hashtag (like ALA), there are thousands of people looking at it. A hashtag is a narrower channel and so you have a lot of people looking at that narrower channel. So, it's easier to find people with similar interests. The hashtags are really the key. And luckily there are a lot of established hashtags. Unluckily, there's, probably a ton of hashtags about other topics that I'm interested in, and libraries that I don't know about. A lot of times if I present at a conference or webinar or not a webinar but a web presentation, I have friends who know my Twitter account who will Tweet that I am doing my presentation. Those are the two biggest ways I get followers, which truly overlap: conferences and presentations.*

- Finish composing your message and click the Tweet button.
- Here are a few things that you should know about adding videos and pictures:
  - Videos do not currently add to your character limit.
  - Twitter supports Mp4 and MOV formats for videos.
  - Videos that are 6.5 seconds or shorter will loop on Twitter.
  - Videos can be sent in direct messages.
  - You can delete a video or a photo by deleting the entire Tweet.
  - Sending a Tweet from an account that is not protected will share the videos and photos in them with the general public.
  - Twitter's mobile app has the capability to include live videos in Tweets.

4.3.9 Identities on Twitter

If you are curious about whether you are truly talking to someone that is a celebrity of some sorts, you can check to see if an account has been verified. Verified accounts have a blue circle or badge with a check mark in the middle (Twitter, 2018c). If the person is truly verified, the symbol will show next to their name on the person's profile page and in search results. If you see a verified badge anywhere else, that means the person put it there themselves and it is a fake. You can review lists of verified accounts by going to the Twitter Verified account (@verified) and reviewing the lists that are available: https://twitter.com/verified. Some names and organizations may not appear on a list. However, you can still see that they are verified. One example is the American Library Association (@AALibrary).

I imagine you might be tempted to request to verify your account. Well, you can't ask. You must be invited. According to Twitter, verified accounts are for high-profile individuals (Twitter, 2018a). Most people are not high profile and will not qualify for a verified account.

If you want to make sure that people know who you are on Twitter, take some measures to share your own information widely. For example, put your Twitter account on your personal website. Put it on your vita or resume. You can also include it on your email signature line. Try posting pictures every so often that authenticate your account. But beware, the more you are on social media and the more important you are, the more likely it is that people will try to hack your account. In this case, follow all of the security measures outlined by Twitter. These measures include using login verification, avoiding third-party apps, and using a secure email address for the account.

4.3.10 How to Create Your Own Moment

- You can create your own Moments in Twitter by clicking on the Moments icon.
- A Create New Moment button will appear at the top of the page.
- Type in a title for the Moment.
- You can select a video or a photo for the cover of the Moment.
- Next add Tweets to the Moment. You can do this by selecting Tweets you have liked, Tweets from your own account, searching for Tweets, or by using a link to a Tweet that you have noticed.
- When you find a Tweet that is suitable, click the check mark next to it to add it to the Moment.
- Sometimes you may not have a video or picture for the cover of the Moment when you start developing it. In this case, begin by adding Tweets to the Moment. The Tweets will automatically populate for viewing in the Set Cover section. Click on the Set cover button again, and you will be able to use one of the Tweets for the cover.
- Select the image and click on the Next button. Then you will be able to crop the image for your cover. Twitter will show you a preview of the image. When you are done cropping the image, click the Next button.
- The preview for the "mobile" view of the page will appear. Crop the image and then click the Save button.
- After the Moment is complete, you can publish it by using the Publish button at the top of the page. Select the Finish Later button to continue developing the Moment in the future.
- If you want to customize your Moment further, use the More button at the top of the page. Use the More button to share your Moment privately, choose the mobile theme color, and tell users that the Moment contains sensitive content. If you have made a mistake on the Moment or no longer want it, you can unpublish or delete it.
- Moments can be shared with a Tweet.

4.3.10.1 Reasons to Use Moments

- You want to have a chat centered around a central topic.
- You have been writing about a topic and want to preserve the Tweets to refer your audience too.
- There is an event that you would like to capture from different perspectives. You can gather the perspectives into a Moment to spark discussion.
- Each week, you want to highlight a topic on Twitter. You pick the best of the Tweets about the topic to create a product like a newsletter.
- You are hosting a live event that you want to promote. A Moment can be used to market the event.
- After an event has started, you can share live videos and photos from the event as a back channel for those who cannot attend.
- When you use a hashtag, someone else may decide that they like it and use it. With a Moment, there is no hashtag. Instead, the content that you have curated is shared in a separate tab.

4.3.11 Finding People to Follow on Twitter

I offer a word of caution before I start to explain how to find people to follow on Twitter. Consider the people that you are adding because the list of people that you follow will also be viewable to everyone who clicks on your page if you have a public account. If you are using Twitter because you want to brand yourself positively, you don't want to follow people who incite hate. Instead, consider searching for them to review their posts. You can also use HootSuite to monitor them. The people who you follow will speak volumes about who you are as a person and the things that are an integral part of your life. Choose wisely.

Twitter offers recommendations for people who you can follow. Click on the Following link while you are in your profiles. If you look at the left side of the page when the new page loads, you will notice a list of people or organizations that seem to fit your preferences. You can refresh the list or click to view all the suggestions. Click the Follow button to add the recommended party to your network. Before following them, consider clicking the name to review their profile. In addition, you can import people from your Gmail account. Click this option and Twitter will search for your contacts. Twitter will ask you for access to your contacts if you have not authorized this.

You can use the search box at the top of the page to find new people to follow. If you are familiar with the name of the individual or organization that you want to follow, search for them. Enter their name in the search box and then click on the hourglass to initiate the search. When you have someone, click on their name to review their profile. Then follow them if you like their profile.

Another way to find people to follow is to look at the profiles of people you admire. While Twitter does offer suggestions based on the people you follow, you may find that by perusing their followers, you can find people who are worthwhile communicating with. Click on the person or organization that you will believe will have interests similar to your own. Next, look at who is following them.

There are also a few websites that give examples of people who are worth following on Twitter. You can complete an influencer search on Klear (www.Klear.com). Besides letting you search Twitter, the website is also good for searching Instagram, YouTube, Blogs, and searching by location. The free plan will give you access to Twitter's basic features. The paid plan offers more detailed results than the free plan.

Searching the Twitter lists of people you admire is also a great way to find new people to follow. Using a Twitter directory is another way to find people and organizations to follow. These websites have directories.
• Twiaholic—http://twitaholic.com/
• Twiends—https://twiends.com/
• TwitterPacks—http://twitterpacks.pbworks.com/w/page/22555521/FrontPage

It is easy to unfollow a person or organization on Twitter. When you feel you are done following someone, simply go back to the list of people you follow and click on their name. When you see their profile page, hover over the Following button. The button will change to Unfollow. Click on it to unfollow them.

4.3.12 Twitter Chats

Twitter may look like a set of comments posted at random times. Yet, it is possible to organize a discussion on Twitter around a designated topic. The answer is to host a Twitter chat. When a group has a Twitter chat, they meet online at a specific time to post Tweets about a predetermined topic. The chat organizer will select and advertise the hashtag for the chat. Then as participants respond, they include the hashtag in their responses.

The organizer poses questions by writing a Q and the question number in front of the question. For example, Question 1 would be Q1. Responses are labeled with an A and the question number. The answer to Question 1 (Q1) would be labeled A1 which represents Answer 1.

4.3.12.1 Following a Chat on Twitter Using the Basic Search
- Do a search for the hashtag you are interested in.
- After the page loads, click the "latest" link at the top of the page.
- Frequently refresh the page to update the conversation.

4.3.12.2 What Are Some Good Things About Twitter Chats?
- You can compile the results and refer to them later.
- You can ask other professionals questions in an informal environment.
- You can create your own professional development experiences and meet new people.
- You can participate from any location.
- You can grow your PLN by tracking who is online.
- You can establish yourself as a leader in your field by addressing a consistent topic.
- You can research a topic.
- You can understand different perspectives on a topic.

4.3.12.3 What Are People Discussing on Twitter Chats?
Here are a few examples:
- New research
- Current events
- Trends in the profession
- Work strategies
- Expert opinions of change agents (panel discussions)
- Announcements regarding new standards
- Q & A sessions about job searches
- How to write a vita or resume
- The tenure and promotion process
- Ethics
- New laws
- Makerspaces and library spaces
- Anything that can improve professional outcomes

4.3.12.4 Finding Chats to Participate In

Your friends might know of chats that are occurring. In addition, if you are following people and notice that they suddenly Tweet out an answer to a question with a hashtag, you can search the hashtag to learn more about that conversation. Furthermore, there are a couple of websites that have lists of Twitter chats to browse. Refer to these websites:

- Tweet Reports: https://www.tweetreports.com/twitter-chat-schedule/
- Education Chats: https://sites.google.com/site/twittereducationchats/education-chat-calendar
- Open Twitter Chat Directory: https://chatdir.kneaver.com/twitter_chats
- Tillison Consulting: https://tillison.co.uk/blog/complete-twitter-chat-hours-directory/

4.3.12.5 Additional Twitter Chat Tips

- Before starting your own chat, observe how other people participate in a chat. What are the things that other moderators do that you like? What are some of the ways that participants react that you find effective?
- Always include the hashtag with your response. This will inform people that you are participating in the chat.
- It is okay to drop in and out of the chat. They are informal, so attend as needed.
- Focus on the topic of the chat. If you would like to discuss something else, make a request to the moderator or start your own chat.
- Look for other people to follow during the chat. Check out their Tweets and decide if they frequently Tweet about topics that you like.
- Remember, if you start a Tweet with a handle, only the people that follow you and the person involved will see the Tweet. Put a word before the handle or put the handle at the end.
- Do some research about the chats that are currently offered. If you find a similar chat on the day that you are interested in having a chat, don't compete with it. Join them instead; participate to get noticed.
- Think about the participants of the chat. Will a certain time be better for them? For example, you would not have a Twitter chat on Sunday morning if you wanted to reach people that attend church. If you are starting a new chat, you should consider putting out a poll to determine the best days and times for the chat.

- When you decide to engage in a Twitter chat, give your followers a clue. Everything that you send during the chat is going to show in their stream. They need to know that they will receive an abundance of Tweets throughout the duration of the chat. Don't be surprised if people unfollow you during a Twitter chat.

4.3.13 Adding Your Location to Tweets

You can add your location to Twitter. There is a GPS icon that shows for each Tweet that you begin to compose. You can disable this feature in the settings. If you want people to know where you are, follow these steps.

- Start a new Tweet.
- Write your Tweet.
- Look at the bottom of the window and click on the GPS icon.
- Twitter will make suggestions about your location.
- Select your location from the drop-down menu or type in a location.
- Send your Tweet.

4.3.14 Additional Twitter Resources

- Hashtag.org (https://www.hashtags.org/)—This member-driven website has a dictionary of hashtags.
- Twitter Chat Infographic (https://create.piktochart.com/output/2617218-library-twitter-chats-2)—This infographic by Easybib shares a list of Twitter chats available for librarians.
- Directory of Twitter Education Chats: https://sites.google.com/site/twittereducationchats/education-chat-official-list.

4.4 YOUTUBE

The About page for YouTube (2018, para. 1) notes that the mission of YouTube is "... to give everyone a voice and show them the world." The company believes that sharing stories is a way to build a global community. Based on this mission, the company promotes the freedom to belong, of opportunity, of information, and expression.

Three former PayPal employees, Chad Hurley, Steve Chen, and Jawed Karem, wanted to create their own startup. Hence, YouTube began as an idea at a dinner party that was sparked by two events in 2004: Janet Jackson's wardrobe malfunction at the Super Bowl and the

Asian tsunami (Hopkins, 2006). It was difficult to find videos of both events. It was then that Karim suggested creating a site on which people could share videos.

Dickey (2013) lists several key events in the company's development. The trademark, logo, and domain for YouTube were filed on February 14, 2005. The beta site was launched by May 2005. The first person to place a video on YouTube was Karim, who shared a short video of himself at the zoo. However, the first video to have millions of views was in September 2005. It was a Nike ad featuring Brazilian soccer player Ronaldinho. Nike's involvement in YouTube was pivotal because Nike was the first company to use YouTube for marketing purposes. YouTube was sold to Google in October 2006. In May 2007, Google introduced a partner program that allowed content creators to make money from their YouTube channels. YouTube entered politics in July 2007 when 7 of the 16 presidential candidates used YouTube to announce their campaigns. The company then collaborated with CNN to host a presidential debate in which candidates answered questions submitted by citizens. By 2009, YouTube was considered to be part of the mainstream when the United States Congress decided to host the Congressional news channel. Since then, YouTube has begun to launch original channels, host live video events, and rent movies. All these events show the power of YouTube as a video sharing website.

According to Jarboe (2012), the popularity of YouTube grew in 2005 when Anthony Padilla and Ian Hecox, both born in 1987, started their YouTube Smosh Channel (www.youtube.com/smosh), with three videos. "The Epic Battle: Jesus vs. Cyborg Satan" amassed well over 20 million views cementing the duo's reputation as YouTube pioneers. Other early YouTubers established YouTube as a place for aspiring film directors to share content. Initially, the audience of YouTube reflected 18-24 year olds. Soon, the YouTube phenomenon caught on as more content creators of various ages focused on developing serious videos. For example, Peter Oakley, born in 1927, also known as the Internet Granddad began sharing his perspectives on life using a YouTube Vlog (video log). Oakley included details about his life that included his war experiences, hobbies, and life after losing a spouse.

Jarboe (2012) notes that YouTube has grown into a mega-platform that hosts TV shows, movies, trailers for movies, hosts contents, and features live events in addition to the content that is available from individual content creators. There are millions of hours of video available on YouTube with at least 8 years of content uploaded each day. All of this is complete with monetized channels and ads that run for sponsors throughout the day. Today, YouTube is a platform for jumpstarting the careers of hopefuls (Dickey, 2013).

YouTube offers several features that can help both blossoming and seasoned professionals. Conceivably, you have used YouTube to view funny videos about the latest trending topics or to occasionally watch a tutorial. You can use YouTube for professional development by searching for thought-leaders who you are already familiar with as a starting point. In addition, you can search for terms in YouTube to help you find related topics. YouTube makes suggestions about videos related to your search terms as well. You can subscribe to channels and curate videos on topics by developing playlists. These features of YouTube help busy professionals to customize their professional development and watch videos on an as-needed basis. I do caution you to verify the information that you watch on YouTube. Some of the information is created by people who are not necessarily credible. YouTube is like other social networks in the way that anyone can create content.

Have you thought about creating your own videos? YouTube has built-in capabilities that make video creation practical and easy when you don't have expensive equipment. If you have a computer, a mic, and a webcam, you can quickly record your own videos to share your opinions and ideas.

YouTube makes having an online presence easier. Millions of people have immediate access to your content. In addition, if your videos are properly tagged and listed, YouTube will show your videos in the search results for people looking for similar topics. YouTube offers the following additional benefits:

- Your audience will understand your persona and speaking skills when you appear in videos.
- You can personalize content for your audience based on their learning preferences. For example, your audience can read a transcript of a video, listen to it, and watch the content.
- YouTube is a quick way to connect with your audience. If they cannot join a live event, they can watch it later.
- YouTube Live can be used for interviews when you don't understand a topic. As such, you are establishing yourself as an expert while you are learning.

Getting started with YouTube is not difficult. You are well on your way if you currently have a Google account. There are a few basics skills that you will need to get started on YouTube. Use these basic tips to get started with using YouTube's features. This section discusses how to upload a video, add captions, change your privacy settings, and create a channel.

4.4.1 How to Upload a Video to YouTube

YouTube allows Google account holders to upload videos. If you don't have an account, go to Gmail.com to sign up.

- Once you have a Google account, go to YouTube.com.
- Click on the Upload icon at the top of the page. It looks like an upward arrow.
- The next screen will prompt you to select the files that you want to upload. You can also drag and drop the files into the designated space in the window.
- Select your privacy choice. Your options include unlisted, public, private, and scheduled. A private video will only be available to you. An unlisted video can be shared with a link. Anyone can see a public video. The scheduled option will allow you to show a video on a certain day and time.
- While your video uploads, you can add a title, description, and tags. YouTube will generate a thumbnail or you can add a custom thumbnail. While you were given the opportunity to check how the video is listed in the last step, you can change it here as well. The video can be added to a playlist too. You can indicate the original language of the video and the language you would like the video to be translated into on the Translations page. Finally, you can make additional changes to your settings on the Advanced settings page. There are settings that include embedding, age restrictions, video statistics, the video category, commenting, and the licenses and rights ownership.
- Wait until the process is completed. While you wait, you will notice that the link for the video is already displayed on the page. You can use this link to share the video with your audience. After YouTube indicates that the processing is complete, select a thumbnail. Then click on Done to confirm the upload. This will publish your content on YouTube. You can also share it on social media, embed, and email the video.

4.4.2 Helpful YouTube Features

Captions: If you truly want to reach all your potential audience members, create captions for your videos. You will want your videos to be accessible. Access the option to add captions by clicking on the Video Manager or your Dashboard to view the videos that you have uploaded. Next click on the Edit button and select Subtitles/CC . There are several ways to work with subtitles and closed captions. For example, you can pay a company to do your captions then upload them. Another option is to write your own script and paste it into YouTube. Finally, YouTube can create automatic captions for your video. If you use the automatic captions, it is always a good practice to go back and edit them. YouTube uses voice recognition and does a great job. However, YouTube may not understand everything that is being said in a video. It will replace the correct words with words that sound similar. This frequently happens when someone has an accent. Three examples of websites that offer transcription and closed caption services are Rev (https://www.rev.com/), Scribe (https://scribie.com/), and 3Play Media (https://www.3playmedia.com/).

Channels: Each channel displays a description and thumbnails of videos that have been publicly shared on the channel. Your videos can go into a YouTube channel. You can have a personal or business channel. If all your content is private or unlisted, content will not be visible to the public on your channel. You can change the settings for your YouTube channel by going to the Creator Studio. There is a link in the menu for the channel in the studio. Note that your personal channel will be slightly different from a business channel. YouTube will automatically prompt you to create a channel when you upload your first video. However, you can make an additional channel with another name for your business. YouTube refers to this as a Brand Account. You can create the additional Brand Account by going to the list of your channels (https://www.youtube.com/channel_switcher) and clicking on the plus sign to create a new channel. Follow the prompts to complete the process.

Analytics: YouTube builds in robust analytics to help market your videos. After all, there is no point in creating videos if you are not going to monitor how they are viewed. You can access your analytics by going to your YouTube Creator Studio. The analytics link will be in the menu. The analytics feature will provide you with data spanning several months so that you can track performance. You are also provided with details that include when your channel was created and what videos you have added to it. Additional functionality and information includes the following:

- The ability to export reports
- The average session duration
- Likes and dislikes
- Comments
- Subscribers
- Demographics
- The location of where videos are played
- The devices that are used to watch your videos

Video Enhancement Options: You don't have to settle for posting plain videos on YouTube. Instead, use the video enhancements tool to quickly customize your videos. Go to your Creator Studio. Click on the Video Manager or your Dashboard to view the videos that you have uploaded. Next click on the Edit button and select Enhancements. You don't need a lot of experience to enhance the videos. Available Enhancements include:

- Auto-fix for lighting and color
- Stabilizing camera movements
- Creating a time lapse
- Applying slow motion
- Trimming the video
- Blurring objects and faces
- Rotating the video

Audio: Unfortunately, you cannot place your favorite song in your videos without first gaining appropriate permission, and doing so can be costly. YouTube helps with this by offering an array of preselected, vetted music to choose from. Click on the Video Manager or your Dashboard to view the videos that you have uploaded. Next click on the Edit button and select Audio. YouTube will display a list of musical selections. You can also visit the YouTube Audio library (https://www.youtube.com/audiolibrary/music) for music and sound effects.

End Screens: Click on the Video Manager or your Dashboard to view the videos that you have uploaded. Next click on the Edit button and select End Screens & Annotations. While the link is for End Screens & Annotations YouTube has discontinued Annotations and replaced them with Cards. End screens provide your viewers with suggestions for videos, playlists, and channels that they can watch on YouTube. End screens also can be used to invite your viewers to sub- scribe to your channel or promote your websites and merchandise. Keep in mind that YouTube has made some changes to the features that are available for end screens. For example, you can mention a website in your video. However, you cannot link to it unless you are a YouTube Partner Program member.

Cards: YouTube cards are designed to add interactivity to videos. Why would you want to add cards? Because there are times, you want to link to other videos, add a call to action, or link to a URL. Currently, YouTube will let you add five cards to videos. Cards are divided into the following categories: Channel, Donation, Link, Poll, and Video or Playlist. Access this feature by clicking on the Video Manager or your Dashboard to view the videos that you have uploaded. Next, click on the Edit button and select Create Card.

YouTube Live Streaming: This is a service that allows you to talk live with an audience by streaming on YouTube. You will need to have a verified channel and make sure that you have not had any live streaming restrictions within the last 90 days on YouTube. See this YouTube Creators course to learn more about live streaming: https://creatoracad- emy.youtube.com/page/course/livestream.

After taking the preliminary steps listed in the course, such as verify- ing your account, you can access live streaming by logging into your Creator Studio. You will see Live Streaming in the Creator Studio menu. The benefit of using live streaming is that your videos will automatically be uploaded to YouTube if they are less than 8 hours in duration. You can then edit and share them. You can set up an event to air in the future or immediately.

4.4.3 Additional Tips

- Vimeo (https://vimeo.com/) is another website that hosts videos for free.
- Make sure that you study the YouTube terms and conditions and con- form to the guidelines.
- Either turn off the comments for videos or monitor them to ensure that offensive comments are not being associated with your videos.

4.5 CONCLUSION

If you are looking for the right way to join a group, or maybe you want to write a creative post for your audience, Twitter, Facebook, and LinkedIn offer functionality to suit all needs. YouTube has several options to help your professional development and assist you with reaching your audience via videos. These options are free and even provide opportunities to earn money from your content. The most important thing to remember about YouTube is that it takes some exploring to learn all the features in-depth. If you are interested, YouTube has an extensive "help" feature that contains step-by-step directions. There is also a course to help you design your new channel. The only thing you have left to do now is to create your first video and to start sharing content online.

The social networks I have described in this chapter offer some amazing ways to write down your ideas, connect with new people, and enjoy a variety of perspectives and content. You can publish information that you want to share with others, and they can react to your posts and connect with you in an instance. You can receive feedback and great ideas to enhance your content. It does not take much effort to get involved with existing groups or to create your own group to grow your PLN. The wide variety of content and ease of use is what makes these networks popular.

4.6 CHAPTER CHALLENGES

4.6.1 LinkedIn

1. Try to acquire 100 contacts on LinkedIn from people that you personally know.
2. Create a publication schedule for your LinkedIn page. What types of topics are relevant to your interests?
3. Join a LinkedIn group and see which topics are discussed the most. Select three topics that you can create content for and write a LinkedIn article.
4. Use one of the free image creation websites listed in Appendix 2 to create your own meme of a hot topic related to your interests.
5. Search for a news article about a topic that is of interest to you. Write your commentary about the topic and monitor the original story and your comments on your social media page.

6. Post an update for your followers at least twice a week and one in a group at least once a week.

4.6.2 YouTube

1. Invite a friend to live stream using Google for an interview. Add closed captions to the discussion and post it on YouTube.
2. Create a playlist of professional development videos to learn about a topic of your choice. Share the playlist with your PLN.
3. Create a tutorial on YouTube about a topic that is important to you. Post the video and market it using another social networking website such as LinkedIn or Facebook.
4. Create a video business card to share when you network at events. Share the link on your regular business card, social media sites, and websites.

4.6.3 Facebook

1. Locate friends who are interested in the same niche as you and invite them to join a private Facebook group.
2. Search for Facebook groups that can help you with your professional development needs.
3. Use Appendix 3 to find US Library Associations to follow on Facebook. Which ones are the most active? Which ones post the best information for professional development purposes?
4. Search Facebook with some of the hashtags listed in Appendix 7. What did you find? Were you able to identify new hashtags via your search?

REFERENCES

Burns, K. S. (2017). *Social Media: A reference handbook.* Santa Barbara, CA: ABC–CLIO.

Dickey, M.R. (February 15, 2013). The 22 key turning points in the history of YouTube. *Business Insider.* Retrieved from ⟨http://www.businessinsider.com/key-turning-points-history-of-youtube-2013-2?op = 1⟩ Accessed 18.01.01.

Hopkins, J. (October 11, 2006). Surprise! There's a third YouTube co-founder. *USA Today.* Retrieved from ⟨http://usatoday30.usatoday.com/tech/news/2006-10-11-you-tube-karim_x.htm⟩ Accessed 18.01.01.

Jarboe, G. (2012). *YouTube and video marketing: An hour a day.* Indianapolis, IN: John Wiley & Sons, Incorporated.

Kessler, G. (December 6, 2016). 'Pizzagate' rumors falsely link death of sex-worker advocate to nonexistent Clinton probe. *The Washington Post.* Retrieved from ⟨https://www.washingtonpost.com/news/fact-checker/wp/2016/12/06/another-false-pizzagate-tale-the-death-of-a-sex-worker-activist-in-haiti/?utm_term = .ee4c4fccf894⟩ Accessed 2017.11.21.

LinkedIn. (2015). *10 words you should not use on your LinkedIn profile.* Retrieved from ⟨https://business.linkedin.com/talent-solutions/blog/2015/01/10-words-you-should-not-use-on-your-linkedin-profile-infographic⟩ Accessed 18.01.15.

LinkedIn. (2016). *LinkedIn company pages-overview.* Retrieved from ⟨https://www.linkedin.com/help/linkedin/answer/28406⟩ Accessed 18.01.15.

Mastrioianni, B. (February 4, 2016). 12 fun facts about Facebook on its 12th birthday. *CBS News.* Retrieved from ⟨https://www.cbsnews.com/media/12-fun-facts-about-facebook-on-its-12th-birthday/⟩ Accessed 18.01.01.

NBC 5 Staff. (July 7, 2016). Sniper ambush kills 5 officers, injures 7 in Dallas following peaceful protest. *NBC 5.* Retrieved from ⟨https://www.nbcdfw.com/news/local/Protests-in-Dallas-Over-Alton-Sterling-Death-385784431.html⟩ Accessed 2017.11.21.

Picard, A. (2017). *The history of Twitter, 140 characters at a time.* Retrieved from ⟨https://www.theglobeandmail.com/technology/digital-culture/the-history-of-twitter-140-characters-at-a-time/article573416/⟩ Accessed 2017.11.21.

Schultz, C. (October 24, 2013). In the wake of the Boston Marathon bombing, Twitter was full of lies. *Smithsonian Magazine.* Retrieved from ⟨https://www.smithsonianmag.com/smart-news/in-the-wake-of-the-boston-marathon-bombing-twitter-was-full-of-lies-5294419/⟩ Accessed 2017.11.21.

Siddiqui, F. & Svrluga, S. (December 5, 2016). N.C. man told police he went to D.C. pizzeria with gun to investigate conspiracy theory. *The Washington Post.* Retrieved from ⟨https://www.washingtonpost.com/news/local/wp/2016/12/04/d-c-police-respond-to-report-of-a-man-with-a-gun-at-comet-ping-pong-restaurant/?utm_term = .2e25173f17fc⟩ Accessed 2017.11.21.

Statista. (2018a). *Most popular social networks worldwide as of January 2018, ranked by number of active users (in millions).* Retrieved from ⟨https://www.statista.com/statistics/272014/global-social-networks-ranked-by-number-of-users/⟩ Accessed 2017.11.21.

Statista. (2018b). *Twitter dossier.* Retrieved from ⟨https://www.statista.com/study/9920/twitter-statista-dossier/⟩ Accessed 2017.11.21.

Twiplomacy. (2017). World leaders with the most Twitter followers as of May 2017. In *Statista—The Statistics Portal.* Retrieved from ⟨https://libproxy.library.unt.edu:9076/statistics/281375/heads-of-state-with-the-most-twitter-followers/⟩ Accessed 2017.11.21.

Twitter. (2018a). *About verified accounts.* Retrieved from ⟨https://help.twitter.com/en/managing-your-account/about-twitter-verified-accounts⟩ Accessed 2017.11.21.

Twitter. (2018b). *Personalization based on where you see Twitter content across the web.* Retrieved from ⟨https://help.twitter.com/en/using-twitter/tailored-suggestions⟩ Accessed 2017.11.21.

Twitter. (2018c). *Verified account FAQs.* Retrieved from ⟨https://help.twitter.com/en/managing-your-account/twitter-verified-accounts⟩ Accessed 2017.11.21.

Van Dijck, J. (2013). *The culture of connectivity: A critical history of social media.* Oxford, England: Oxford University Press.

YouTube.com. (2018). *About.* Retrieved from ⟨https://www.youtube.com/yt/about/⟩ Accessed 18.01.01.

FURTHER READING

BBC News. (2015). *Fake LinkedIn profiles used by hackers.* Retrieved from ⟨http://www.bbc.com/news/technology-34994858⟩ Accessed 18.01.15.

eMarketer. (2018). Number of Twitter users worldwide from 2014 to 2020 (in millions). In *Statista—The Statistics Portal*. Retrieved from ⟨https://libproxy.library.unt. edu:9076/statistics/303681/twitter-users-worldwide/⟩ Accessed 2017.11.21.

Palmer, D. (July 27, 2017). How these fake Facebook and LinkedIn profiles tricked people into friending state-backed hackers. *ZD Net*. Retrieved from ⟨http://www. zdnet.com/article/how-these-fake-facebook-and-linkedin-profiles-tricked-people-into-friending-state-backed-hackers/⟩ Accessed 18.01.15.

Roth, C. (January 13, 2017). How to keep yourself safe from fake LinkedIn profiles. *Entrepreneur*. Retrieved from ⟨https://www.entrepreneur.com/article/287398⟩ Accessed 18.01.15.

CHAPTER 5

Automating Your Social Media

Figure 5.1 People discussing social media.

5.1 RSS FEEDS

RSS feeds were present before social media. According to Burns (2017), they began as a way to facilitate blogging in 1999. RSS stands for "Really Simple Syndication" or "Rich Site Summary" depending on who defines it. RSS feeds are credited as a creation of Dave Winer. RSS feeds are beneficial because they segment data into themes that can be broadcasted on the Internet. Website owners use RSS feeds to share blog posts, news, and other content online through an aggregator. An aggregator is a program that can check an RSS feed for new information and post it online. An aggregator can gather information from various websites. Sometimes aggregators are referred to as RSS readers (Gil, 2017). (See Table 5.1 for a list of free RSS readers.)

Growing Your Library Career with Social Media
DOI: https://doi.org/10.1016/B978-0-08-102411-9.00005-4

Table 5.1 Free RSS readers

RSS reader	Link
Feedly	https://feedly.com/i/welcome
Digg Reader	http://digg.com/reader
NewsBlur	https://newsblur.com/
The Old Reader	https://theoldreader.com/

Many assumed that RSS feeds would become obsolete when Google discontinued the Google Reader in 2013 (Baker, 2017) because the company felt the service's usage declined (Google, 2013). However, RSS feeds remain a viable resource for mining web content (Baker, 2017; Sutherland, 2016). While many libraries and individual librarians use social media to manage content, RSS feeds still have a place for aggregating online materials.

RSS feeds let you search websites to stay up-to-date on current information (Gil, 2017). They are excellent for some users because of their browsing capabilities. Readers can automate the search process and put the requested information in a minimalist web environment (Baker, 2017). Once a reader is selected and formatted, it is easy to peruse readings.

Using an RSS reader has other benefits. For example, a search can yield results with research highlights, summaries of journal content, articles and blog posts about a topic of interest, job opportunities, and news about trending topics (NYU Libraries, 2017). See Appendix 6, Blogs for Librarians for a list of blogs that include RSS feeds relevant to library and information science.

5.1.1 The Basics of Subscribing to an RSS Feed

Subscribing to an RSS feed is free and easy. Like websites, RSS feeds have their own links. I will share one method for subscribing to RSS feeds. While there are many RSS readers to choose from, I will use Feedly for this example. The process should be similar to the RSS reader that you select. Here are the steps.

1. Subscribe to the RSS reader Feedly.
2. Log into your account.
3. Go to a website with an RSS feed that you would like to subscribe to such as the Latest News feed from the Library of Congress (http://www.loc.gov/rss/pao/news.xml).

4. Go back to your RSS reader account website.
5. Paste the link into the RSS reader and click on enter.
6. Click on your result to subscribe. In Feedly, this requires clicking on the Follow button in the right-hand corner of the page.
7. A "pop up" will state, "To follow this source, create a new feed." Click on, + New Feed.
8. When your content begins to appear, hover over the titles to bookmark them to read later, mark as read, and delete them.
9. When the dialog box opens, give the feed a name and click on the Create button.

Now you can enjoy your content on your computer and devices. Keep in mind that you can search inside of Feedly using keywords, hashtags, Twitter handles, and URLs. The basic version of Feedly is free. It includes 100 sources, 3 RSS feeds, and 3 boards.

You can curate information by saving it to a board. A curation is a collection of information items. Save various articles to a board by clicking the star next to them. Feedly (2017) explains that boards are a great way to keep content organized. Each board can have a unique name. Any item that you have opened on Feedly can be shared on social media by using one of the share buttons. If you like extensions, you can use the Feedly browser extension for Chrome, Firefox, or Safari to add articles while you surf the Internet.

5.1.2 Final Thoughts on RSS Feeds

Now that you have signed up for your RSS reader, it is time to enjoy the bounty of your efforts. It is true that RSS feeds are not necessarily social media. However, you can use them with social media. Start by looking at the headings of the articles and determine what you need to do to make yourself relevant to the current trends. For example, LIS News (LISNews.org) created a post called the "Ten Stories that Shaped 2017". Naturally, true to the tagline of the publication "Scandalous Since 1999," the post contained topics that were controversial in LIS (LIS News, 2017). The stories included "Librarians Fight Fake News," "ALA's Trump Statements," and "The Opioid Crisis."

Many of these topics are social justice related. As librarians interweave their way between serving the interest of the public and providing environments that make everyone feel welcome, these are hot topics that are sure to spark conversation. The question is, do you want to engage in the conversation? Linking to the stories and making comments on the posts of this nature can positively impact how people see you as an expert. Controversial topics often get a lot of "hits" and responses on social media. You can take a side or offer a discussion that explains how the two sides can work together. Or you can simply repost the information for other readers to view. In this way, re-posting the topics can increase your visibility because you are offering timely information. You could be the individual that contributes the voice of reason to the conversation. Just be sure to carefully research the topic before you speak about it. You want to be well informed.

5.2 IF THIS THEN THAT

It is the end of the day, and you have a deadline approaching. You have written a great blog post, but it needs to be shared on your Facebook, Twitter, and blog pages. While these tasks are easy, it takes some time to log into each website to complete them. Also, it is annoying and counter-productive to complete repetitive tasks. However, it cannot be avoided because you have followers on each of the websites. Is there anything that you can do to make the best of your time? The answer is yes. Automate your tasks. Websites that can do this include If This Then That (IFTTT) and HootSuite.

According to Hoy (2015), an automated task service website enables users to program triggers to allow data to flow from one website to another. Users control this flow of information by defining the rules that signal when data should be transferred. Hoy (2015, p. 99) provides these examples of tasks that can be automated.

- Automate the uploading of photos or documents from one web service to another.
- Duplicate postings on numerous social media sites.
- Create social media posts from uploaded photos or documents.
- Gather articles and social media posts that contain keywords and reblog them or track them in a spreadsheet.

While there are many different services, each one has one thing in common. They are based on a trigger that causes an action. For example, if someone mentions you on a website using your tag (trigger), then the service can be programmed to send you a reminder to contact them (Hoy, 2015).

Hoy (2015) notes that some users have security concerns about using automated task services. Before one can use them, they must authorize the service to access their social media accounts. This requires users to sign an agreement and to enter their password for the social media accounts that will be accessed.

If one can overcome security concerns, outside of growing your career with social media, you might find IFTTT suitable for other tasks in the real world. For example, when writing about IFTTT, Weber (2017) states,

> Described in this column is a type of automation not originally considered beyond industrial robots deployed to efficiently and economically assemble everything from automobiles to smartphones. The connection between our desires or intentions--and the services we need or want--has only just begun. (p. 49)

While humans may have envisioned robots that completed simple tasks such as putting together cars, computers have evolved and are much more integrated into our lives. The potential for more uses continues to grow each year. Weber explains that IFTTT can connect to devices such as smartphones, Alexa, and TV remotes. The service can be used to find devices when they are lost, connect to a security system to automatically lock doors at a specific time, or start Google Maps navigation 15 minutes before a trip.

Linden Tibbets, the founder of IFTTT.com, made his first blog post about the service in 2010. In the post, Tibbett referred to the service as, "Digital duct tape if you will, allowing you to connect any two services together" (Tibbets, 2010, para. 8). Since its inception in 2014, the service has evolved. The company has developed ways to connect "ordinary objects to online services" (Newman, 2016, para. 14). Instead of focusing on using developer tools, the service now has relationships with partners such as car, television, and utility companies.

5.2.1 Getting Started with IFTTT

IFFTT works by using applets to connect services. IFTTT (2018, para. 1) states, "Services are the apps and devices you use every day." An IFTTT service can be turned on by using an app. I currently use IFTTT to find mentions of hashtags on Twitter about educational technology. I am responsible for teaching on this topic and need to stay up-to-date. When I have time, I go to my Google account, and I read the Tweets that are in the spreadsheet. While you can set up many activities in IFTTT, I will use adding Tweets to a spreadsheet as an example. Then you will be able to explore additional options in the future.

5.2.2 IFTTT Applets

After signing up, when you click on the My Applets page, you will see a button to create a New Applet. If you click Discover link at the top of your IFTTT homepage, a new page will load with a variety of recommended applets. You will see that these applets are made by IFTTT, partners like Google, and IFTTT users. IFTTT will display how many users are currently using each applet. More applets will load as you scroll down the page. If you click on one, you can turn it on. Then IFTTT will provide a series of prompts to follow to set up the applet.

5.2.3 The Search Page

You can also use the search page to find new applets. Click on the Search icon at the top of the page. When the page loads, you will see a search box, applets recommended for you, and categories of applets. The applet categories are alphabetized, and social media (i.e., social network) is toward the bottom of the page. If you click on the All Services link below the categories, you will be taken to a page that lists every service under each category. Some of the social media categories include applications, blogging, calendars and scheduling, bookmarking, email, education, and social media.

5.2.4 Setting Up an Applet

This is an example of how to set up an applet. In this example, I will have IFTTT search for Tweets about personal branding.

- Start by clicking the applet. This one is called, Save Tweets Featuring Specific Content to a Spreadsheet. It was created by Google and works with Twitter. After you select the applet, it will take you to a page where you can turn it on.
- The next page that loads is the Configuration page. You can choose to receive notifications when the applet runs. If you do this, I recommend setting up a folder in your email account to receive the notifications. The Configuration page serves two purposes. It allows you to set up the applet or change it after it has been set up. The Configuration page will show right after you decide to set up a new applet and when you decide to edit one.

- If you find that you have an applet that you no longer need, you can edit or delete it. Start by clicking on the icon that looks like a cogwheel in the right-hand corner of the applet.

When you click on the cogwheel for this applet, a page will load with various options for changes. Configurations will vary according to the applet that you have decided to create or use. You can:

- Decide to get notifications.
- Decide what to search for.
- Add rows to a spreadsheet after a Tweet.
- Format how the rows display.
- Select the folder where the spreadsheet is placed.
- Save your choices.
- If you don't want to keep the applet, click on Delete to eliminate it. This option is at the bottom of the applet.

5.2.5 IFTTT Activity Page

You can monitor activities inside of IFTTT by clicking on the activity page. For example, if you are using IFTTT to search for Twitter hashtags, it will show you a page listing the actions that were taken. In this example, I searched for #edtech. The activity page shows me details that include the link to the Tweet that was added to the spreadsheet, the text of the Tweet, code to embed the Tweet, the URL for the author's image, and the author's username.

5.2.6 Create Your Own Applet

You can build your own applets with IFTTT. Follow these directions to accomplish the task.

- Start by going to your username at the top right-hand side of the page.
- Next, click on the arrow to access the drop-down menu.
- Select New Applet from the menu.
- When the page loads, click on the + this part of the text on the page.
- Next, choose the service that you want to use for the applet. I will continue to use Twitter since we started with it. My Twitter account is already connected. But you will have to follow the prompts to give IFTTT access to your account.

- After you authorize access to your account, you will be taken to Step 2 to choose a trigger or action that you want to take place for the applet.
- I have decided that I would like to look at Tweets by @ACRL, which is the Association of College and Research Libraries (ACRL).
- I have typed in the @ACRL username. Now I will click on the Create Trigger button.
- The next step is the "then + that" stage. Click on the + that part of the text on the screen. In this case, it appears in blue.
- Now it is time to choose a service. I want to use Twitter again because I plan to resend the @ACRL Tweets.
- I choose to Post a Tweet.
- Next, I choose the button to Add ingredient and select the LinktoTweet option. I am done adding ingredients.
- My next step is to click on the Create Action button.
- The applet is complete. Click on the Finish button. You should also decide if you want to receive notifications when the applet runs.

Now you have a new applet. Wait for it to run. Then check the results. Be careful about what you post. Once it goes online, you may delete it. Yet, there is always the possibility that content can be captured on a website which archives the Internet. You can look at your Twitter account and use your activity page to monitor the content.

5.2.7 Final Thoughts on If This Then That

IFTTT makes it easy to automate your social networking and other activities in your life. I am sure you can also see the benefit of using it for personal branding and automating your online professional development. Think of it this way. You can program IFTTT to find and populate spreadsheets with the most current discussions about topics that are important to you. You can find people to follow and have IFTTT to make it easy to follow them. If you want a reminder to thank someone for mentioning your post, IFTTT has it covered. If you are going to monitor your reputation online, let IFTTT find who is mentioning you and what they are saying. Then get a map to show up to your next speaking engagement.

In addition, keeping up with what you post online can be tedious. IFTTT is well equipped for this task. You can set IFTTT to Tweet about posts pertaining to a particular topic, or you can find blog posts to summarize for your next post. There are millions of applets to try. All you need to do is explore your options.

5.3 HOOTSUITE

A concern for many people when they begin using social media is whether they will have the time to maintain it. This may be even more true for people who have multiple accounts, including both personal and professional accounts, for social media platforms. For example, you may use LinkedIn to follow professional development events using one username, then switch to Facebook to communicate with family and friends. Switching between accounts can be daunting and increases the risk of posting something to the wrong account. Can you imagine posting a personal message to your professional account (Box 5.1)?

HootSuite is a solution to help manage this situation. HootSuite is a social media dashboard system for brand management and the promotion of individuals, Internet-based, and non Internet-based companies. HootSuite provides integration with the major social networking websites, like Facebook, Myspace, Twitter, LinkedIn, and Google + . The free version of HootSuite lets you connect three social media platforms. Perhaps you have more; if that's the case, choose your most important platforms. HootSuite provides a simple way to manage what you are doing online. Because it serves as a dashboard, you do not have to navigate from one website to another to complete your tasks. It also provides applications for tracking and monitoring your activities so that you can

BOX 5.1 How do you organize your social media accounts?

Ayla Stein—I don't keep that many. I usually use hashtags for Twitter. I save a lot of them as lists or save pictures. And I like to use hashtags on HootSuite. I think HootSuite has the best set-up for having dedicated feeds for different hashtags. I have lists on Facebook. I keep them all automated.

I've also used If This Then That, (IFTTT), I like to use that to, create automated back-ups of Tweets, Also, whenever the President signs a new law into, I have a managed recording of that.

There is not too much overlap between my friends on my Facebook and Twitter accounts. I avoid knowing people that I know in person on Tumblr. Tumblr is basically just for nerdy stuff.

determine if what you are doing is effective so that you can make better decisions.

For example, if you are using multiple social media platforms, you might want to determine if the latest platform that you are using is worth your time. You can use HootSuite to measure your audience's response to the information that you are posting. This is effective for busy professionals that do not want to waste their time. Moreover, using HootSuite to look for key phrases can help you with your professional development. All your information is gathered in one space to help you determine your next move.

You can also use HootSuite to monitor conferences and events. Just find out what the conference hashtags are. Many conferences now offer a backchannel to stay abreast of what it is happening. In this instance, if you are attending the conference, you can share what you are learning. On the contrary, if you are unable to attend, you can still benefit from it by using the conference backchannel and gleaning useful information from the attendees.

You can also locate thought leaders with HootSuite. Just enter your favorite hashtag or phrase. Then monitor the conversation to determine who is speaking about the topic the most. When they post, try to comment on what they write. In addition, try following them if the conversation is meaningful to you. Sometimes people will follow you back if you start following them. Just make sure that when you post, you are saying something that others might find thought-provoking. Posting interesting material that matches current trends will increase your number of followers.

Here are some other things that HootSuite can allow you to do:

- Watch multiple social media networks on one page.
- Get basic statistics about your social media posts and monitor traffic. You can pay for additional analytics if you would like more detail.
- Write several social media posts within HootSuite.
- Schedule your social media posts if you believe you are going to be busy. Consistent posts will give your audience consistent exposure to your ideas.
- Post the same information to multiple platforms.
- Perform searches for key terms and hashtags.
- Monitor your mentions on social media platforms.

HootSuite can be managed in columns for different accounts. For example, you can make columns for mentions on social media, for messages that you have sent, or for keywords that you want to search. It is much easier to block out unwanted social media noise when you develop a strategy for monitoring the information you are interested in. In this way, you can make your social media activity work for you, rather than you working to use social media in a proactive manner.

HootSuite is designed to grow with your brand. If you find that you need to collaborate with a team, the paid versions of HootSuite will allow you to have multiple people monitoring one account. Each person can be assigned different streams to watch. Moreover, multiple people can check to see if material is accurate before it is posted to the Internet.

5.3.1 Final Thoughts on HootSuite

Even though you are busy, monitoring social media does not have to be a burden. Use a social media dashboard, such as HootSuite, to improve your productivity. HootSuite is an application that offers multiple ways to tackle your social media tasks. It is an in-depth website with many layers of services. Stop monitoring your social media networks separately and get smarter about how you spend your time. Look at HootSuite's quick start guide today.

5.4 SCOOP.IT

Social media conversations and Internet content change rapidly. Sometimes, it is hard to come up with new content every day. That is where a website like Scoop.it can be helpful to you. Not only does Scoop.it generate content, it organizes content into a nice format for your audience to read. It also curates information from the Internet so that you do not have to continually search for the topics that you need to learn about. Simply stated, Scoop.it is a great way to keep your audience informed while you stay up-to-date on the latest topics. Digital curation through websites like Scoop.it allows you to build your reputation, drives traffic to your sites, and it also makes it easier for you to generate interest from your audience.

Conversely, Scoop.it is a platform that is easy to use. That makes it a lot simpler for you to obtain quality content. It is designed to help you maintain a connection to your audience. Since Scoop.it allows you to publish your content on social media, you will be able to set up the target platform automatically. You can distribute your curated content directly to sites such as Twitter, Facebook, LinkedIn, and WordPress. Scoop.it offers a free and paid version. Regardless of the version that is chosen, it is well worth your attention.

5.4.1 How Can You Use Scoop.it?

Signing up for Scoop.it is a quick process. Go to https://www.scoop.it/ and follow the prompts to create an account. If you don't want to use your Twitter or Facebook account, use an email address to create the account instead.

Once you have access to the website, the first thing you need to do in Scoop.it is to add a topic that is relevant to your niche. The website will guide you through settings up your topic. While you are not writing the content, focusing on your niche will remind your audience that you are an expert. Think of some keywords that compliment your topic and type them in.

5.4.2 Configuring Scoop.it

Once you have set up your search, it is necessary to know how to manage it to get the best results. The advanced configuration window allows you to add extra keywords aside from the ones you searched for. You will be able to set an option where you can see posts limited to a specific time period. I recommend setting the time to 1 month to keep the information on your page current.

The filtering options also enable you to filter suggestions based on articles, documents, videos, social networks, and pictures. You can limit searches to the titles or URLs. As you get results, you will notice that Scoop.it will show the number of shares a page received on social media. This means you get to see what articles are popular and use them to drive traffic to your sites.

5.4.3 Publishing Scoop.it Results

You must select a destination for your posts. You can have your posts published on your Scoop.it topic page, as well as social media networks. The free version currently allows connections to two networks. As you click to "scoop" each article, you will be invited to share your insight about them. You can share the image and add tags. When you are done, click on the Publish button to share the post.

5.4.4 Analytics

Scoop.it lets you track your page. You can review your curated scoops, the topics you are following, and who is following your scoops. Scoop.it will also form a community for you. The community consists of curators that you are following on Scoop.it, or if you have connected your social media profiles, it will contain the people that are linked to you on other social media websites. You can also see how many views you have received in a day. Of course, the paid version of Scoop.it will provide more details.

5.4.5 Improving Your Content

Scoop.it has a bookmarklet for curation. There is also a suggestion engine for scanning the content. One thing to keep in mind is that you can optimize your results by adding your own sources if you want to curate content more efficiently!

5.4.6 Scoop.it Tips

Scoop.it is one of the best content curation tools available. Other digital curation tools include Paper.li and Pearltrees. See Appendix 4 for additional options. Remember, your results can be surprising if you take the time to read the content and develop your keywords. Get the most out of Scoop.it by searching for terms that can improve your career and complement your niche. You want to learn as you share.

- Don't copy an entire post because you need to give credit to the creator.
- Always try out new keywords to find diverse content.
- Preview the content to check for quality.

5.5 CHAPTER CHALLENGES

1. Search IFTTT for new applets that match the social networking sites that you use.
2. Try two new applets from IFTTT to automate your posts from one social media site to another.
3. Set up an IFTTT applet to monitor an organization or social media superstar for your professional development.
4. Use HootSuite and type in a search term for a topic that you are interested in. What is the difference between typing in a hashtag with

a term and typing a term without a hashtag? After a day, go back to your HootSuite account. What type of new information did you learn from your HootSuite search? Are you able to identify new thought leaders that you want to follow?

5. Browse Scoop.It to determine if there is anyone posting in your content area. If you find someone with a similar interest, how can you make your posts different? In addition, what types of posts are you able to find that can help you with your professional development?

6. Look at the blogs in Appendix 6. Find three blogs related to your topic of choice and set up RSS feeds. How do the blogs that you have selected address the topic differently?

REFERENCES

Baker, J. (2017). *5 open source RSS feed readers*. Retrieved from ⟨https://opensource.com/article/17/3/rss-feed-readers⟩ Accessed 2017.12.27.

Burns, K. S. (2017). *Social media: A reference handbook*. Santa Barbara, CA: ABC-CLIO.

Feedly. (2017). *Introducing boards, notes, and highlights*. Retrieved from ⟨https://blog.feedly.com/boards/⟩ Accessed 2017.12.27.

Gil, P. (2017). How RSS works and why you should use it. *Lifewire*. Retrieved from ⟨https://www.lifewire.com/what-is-rss-2483592⟩ Accessed 2017.12.27.

Google. (2013). *A second spring of cleaning*. Retrieved from ⟨http://googleblog.blogspot.com/2013/03/a-second-spring-of-cleaning.html⟩ Accessed 2017.12.27.

Hoy, M. B. (2015). If this then that: An introduction to automated task services. *Medical Reference Services Quarterly*, *34*(1), 98–103. Available from https://doi.org/10.1080/02763869.2015.986796.

IFTTT. (2018). *About*. Retrieved from https://ifttt.com/about Accessed 2018.01.15.

LIS News. (2017). *Ten stories that shaped 2017*. Retrieved from ⟨http://lisnews.org/ten_stories_that_shaped_2017⟩ Accessed 2017.12.27.

Newman, J. (2016). *Inside IFTTT's plan for a more harmonious Internet*. Retrieved from ⟨https://www.fastcompany.com/3065864/inside-ifttts-plan-for-a-more-harmonious-internet⟩ Accessed 2017.12.27.

NYU Libraries. (2017). *RSS: Making information come to you*. Retrieved from ⟨https://guides.nyu.edu/rss⟩ Accessed 2017.12.27.

Sutherland, M. (2016). *The crux of a social media strategy*. Code{4}lib Journal. Issue 31. Retrieved from ⟨http://journal.code4lib.org/articles/11299⟩ Accessed 2017.12.27.

Tibbets, L. (2010). *IFTTT the beginning*. Retrieved from ⟨https://ifttt.com/blog/2010/12/ifttt-the-beginning⟩.

Weber, R. M. (2017). Computer, make me a malted. *Journal of Financial Service Professionals*, *71*(6), 47–50.

CHAPTER 6

Copyright Considerations

Figure 6.1 Copyright concept on tablet PC.

6.1 INTRODUCTION

We all know that copyright law is serious business. Infringing on someone else's intellectual property can have serious consequences that include paying huge fines and going to jail. Here is a quick review of copyright law basics to assist you with following the law while you are posting on social media.

Copyright law is a constitutional law which automatically offers legal protection to the original work of authors. This law offers protection to their original works by prohibiting public and private use without obtaining or being granted the formal permission to use such items. Basically, copyright law bestows the exclusive legal right, for the author of a creative work, to control the copying of a work (Templeton, 2008). Copyright law grants the author of an original piece legal rights and protection to their work, which includes the right to publish, reproduce, sell, display, prepare derivative works of, and perform the work for a limited period.

1. You cannot copyright an idea or fact. However, you can copyright the way that the idea is implemented.

Growing Your Library Career with Social Media
DOI: https://doi.org/10.1016/B978-0-08-102411-9.00006-6

2. If you publish an original work alone, the copyright lasts for your entire life plus 70 years.
3. Under some circumstances, you can leave your copyright to someone using a will, or you can transfer your rights.
4. You cannot include a copyrighted work in your own work and claim a new copyright on it. The existing copyright remains intact.
5. Copyright begins as soon as an original work is fixed to a tangible form. Tangible forms can include but are not limited to, recordings, books, and emails.
6. Although copyright is applied to an original work once it is in a tangible form, registering the work adds another layer of legal protection.
7. If a company pays you and you create a work specifically for them, you do not own the copyright, and the company does.
8. A work published before 1923 is in the public domain.
9. A copyright notice tells people that you are the copyright owner and you have claimed ownership of a document. It includes the following:
   a. The copyright system or the word "copyright."
   b. The year of publication or creation of documents that have not been published.
   c. The name of the owner, title, or term that clearly indicates who the owner is.
10. According to the U.S. Copyright Office (2017, p. 1), the following items are protected by copyright laws:
   a. Literary works
   b. Musical works, including any accompanying words
   c. Dramatic works, including any accompanying music
   d. Pantomimes and choreographic works
   e. Pictorial, graphic, and sculptural works
   f. Motion pictures and other audiovisual works
   g. Sound recordings, which are works that result from the fixation of a series of musical, spoken, or other sounds
   h. Architectural works

Fair Use offers exceptions to copyright law under specific conditions. Fair Use is defined as, "a legal doctrine that promotes freedom of expression by permitting the unlicensed use of copyright-protected works in certain circumstances" (U.S. Copyright Office, 2017, p. 6). For example, educators can distribute a certain number of copies of a copyrighted work. The use of the copyrighted material must be for education. Moreover, it is important for those invoking Fair Use to be careful not to give away the essence of the copyright material or make too many copies. Using a work cannot negatively impact sales and the generation of income from the work. There are several nuances to copyright and Fair Use which make it the subject of several debates. See Appendix 10, created by the Association for Research Libraries for an infographic about Fair Use myths and facts.

While copyright laws exist in the United States, there are no provisions for international copyright. How copyright is implemented in respective countries depends on the laws of the country. Some countries do have international copyright agreements with the United States. Regardless of whether a country has an agreement with the United States or not, it is vital to understand that U.S. copyright laws have a mandatory deposit provision. The rule notes that two of the best copies of a work must be sent to the Library of Congress. The purpose of this rule is to ensure that the library maintains copies of every copyrighted document in the United States.

To ensure that you do not infringe upon someone else's rights and you know how to protect your own rights, visit the U.S. Copyright Office's website. The website has an extensive collection of flyers and is helpful for determining how to adhere to copyright laws.

6.2 CREATIVE COMMONS LICENSE CONDITIONS

Understanding Creative Commons Licenses is another aspect of understanding copyright. Rather than using the traditional copyright affordances, one can assign a Creative Commons license to their work. With traditional copyright, all rights are reserved. On the contrary, with a Creative Commons license, creative works can be assigned to the public domain with a CC0 license or use a combination of options to maintain that some rights are reserved (Creative Commons, 2018). Many authors are gravitating toward using Creative Commons licenses to facilitate the distribution of their work. There are a variety of Creative Commons conditions and licenses that can be applied to creative works. This section will explain them based on the definitions provided by Creative Commons (2018).

6.2.1 Attribution (BY)

All Creative Commons licenses dictate that any individuals who use the work you have created in any way, shape, or form must ensure you are appropriately credited for your efforts in the way in which you specify but not in a manner that indicates you endorse their use of your work. If others wish to use something you have created without explicitly crediting you, they must first gain your permission to do so.

6.2.2 ShareAlike (SA)

The ShareAlike license condition specifies that you give others permission to reproduce, distribute, modify, perform, or display something you have created on the proviso they distribute any modified version of your work on the same terms. If others wish to distribute modified versions of your work under alternative conditions, they must first gain your permission to do so.

6.2.3 NonCommercial (NC)

The NonCommercial license condition specifies that you give others permission to reproduce, distribute, modify (unless you have specified NoDerivatives), perform, or display something you have created provided it is not used for commercial purposes. If others wish to use your work for commercial purposes, they must first gain your permission to do so.

6.2.4 NoDerivatives (ND)

The NoDerivatives license condition specifies that you give others permission to reproduce, distribute, perform, or display something you have created. However, if they wish to modify your work, they must first gain your permission to do so.

6.3 TYPES OF LICENSES

Combining the conditions results in several types of licenses. Here is an overview of each type of license.

6.3.1 Attribution CC BY

The Attribution CC BY license permits third parties to share, modify, add to, and reproduce your work for personal or commercial purposes on the proviso you are appropriately credited for your efforts. This license is the most accommodating of the licenses that are currently in use. It is suitable for those who are seeking the maximum distribution and application of licensed materials.

6.3.2 Attribution ShareAlike CC BY-SA

This license allows others to reproduce, distribute, modify, perform, or display something you have created on the proviso that they distribute any modified version of your work on the same terms. If others wish to distribute modified versions of your work under alternative conditions, they must first gain your permission to do so. This license is very similar to "copyleft" free and open source software licenses. When you apply this restriction, any new works that were based on your previous efforts will carry the same license; as such, derivatives of the work will also be available for commercial use. Wikipedia currently uses the CC BY-SA license, and it is suitable for any works that stand to benefit from integrating material from Wikipedia and projects that operate under a similar license.

6.3.3 Attribution-NoDerivs CC BY-ND

This license gives others permission to redistribute your content for noncommercial or commercial purposes providing it is not modified in any way and you are credited for the work.

6.3.4 Attribution-NonCommercial CC BY-NC

This license permits others to reproduce, distribute, modify, perform, or display something you have created provided it is not used for commercial purposes. However, while any new works that are derived from your work must also be limited to noncommercial purposes and acknowledge your work, derivative works do not need to be licensed on the same terms.

6.3.5 Attribution-NonCommercial-ShareAlike CC BY-NC-SA

This license allows others to reproduce, distribute, modify, perform, or display something you have created provided it is not used for commercial purposes and derived works are licensed under the identical terms.

6.3.6 Attribution-NonCommercial-NoDerivs CC BY-NC-ND

This is the most restrictive license. Under this license, users are only permitted to download and share your works with others under the agreement that you are given full credit. They are not permitted to modify the works in any way or to use them for commercial purposes.

6.4 CONCLUSION

In conclusion, as you use social media, information that is posted on the Internet is protected by copyright law. Being a responsible consumer and producer of information dictates understanding copyright rules and how to apply them. Today, authors are not bound by traditional copyright and explore additional Creative Commons Licenses to facilitate the dissemination of their work. Regardless of the type of copyright that is chosen, properly applying copyright law will help you to protect your personal brand.

6.5 CHAPTER CHALLENGES

1. Examine the Creative Commons licenses. Are there any that you would use for your work? Why or why not?
2. Several websites use Creative Commons licenses. One example is Boundless (https://courses.lumenlearning.com/catalog/boundlesscourses). Look at the resources that are available on the website and determine if there are any that you could remix to help you further your brand.
3. OER Commons (https://www.oercommons.org/) is another website that offers content shared with Creative Commons licenses. Develop a resource to place on the OER Commons site and share it on your social networking sites.

REFERENCES

Creative Commons. (2018). Frequently asked questions. Retrieved from ⟨https://creativecom-mons.org/faq/#what-is-creative-commons-and-what-do-you-do⟩ (accessed 2018.01.21).
Templeton, B. (2008). 10 big myths about copyright explained. Retrieved from ⟨http://www.templetons.com/brad/copymyths.html⟩ (accessed 2018.01.21).
U.S. Copyright Office. (2017). Copyright basics. Retrieved from ⟨https://www.copy-right.gov/circs/circ01.pdf⟩ (accessed 2018.01.21).

CHAPTER 7

Creating Content

Figure 7.1 Idea text on a screen.

Now that you know about various social media platforms, it is time for you to start posting your own content. Creating customized content for your audience will establish you as an expert. This chapter provides tips for creating content that will be engaging to followers regardless of the social media network that you are using.

Think about the personal brand that you are trying to develop. With your personal brand in mind, offer something helpful that is important for people to know. What problems need to be solved? What situations are people apprehensive about addressing?

Publish consistent content that shows expertise about specific topics. When people look at your information online, what will they know about it before they read it? For example, on a given week, one of your followers may know that you will post a comment or story about a new type of technology that is relevant to libraries (Box 7.1).

Use all types of media and cross-post the information. You can use videos, newsletters, Twitter posts, Facebook posts, and LinkedIn content. Be consistent with your posts. If this is a problem, you might consider using a tool such as HootSuite. Schedules options can include:

- Once a week
- Once a day or twice a day
- Just on the weekend

BOX 7.1 How do you maintain your followers on social media?

kYmberly Keeton—I have always been consistent with my content. I post about librarianship, writing, art, and social politics, as well as my daily rants on Facebook. I use LinkedIn for all of my career pursuits. I use Twitter as a place to be spunky and have a little flavor to my writing. I use Instagram for everything that I do. Honestly, I believe my work, my writing, and my images are thought-provoking and make people think and that is how I have a pretty nice following with all of my social media platforms.

BOX 7.2 How often do you post on social media?

Dr. Jason Alston—I try to Tweet at least three times a day. Not all of those are going to be professional Tweets. At least every other day, I try to have some sort of professional Tweet. I never want to go a full day without Tweeting anything.

Greg Hardin—I post about twice a week on Twitter. On Facebook I post more. I have a lot of library-like friends. It's not open or public. But most of the content on there tends to be library related unless friends or family kind of tag me in their holiday picture or something like that.

Look at the schedule of your followers. Try posting for a few weeks at specific time intervals. For example, you might post at 10:00 a.m., 2:00 p.m., and 6:00 p.m. During which times are people more likely to respond to or view your content? Use their responses to establish a schedule. Again, you don't have to be at your computer to post during these times. Instead, schedule your posts (Box 7.2).

Try linking to other comments and stories. When you link to content, make sure that you are making a comment about it. If you don't make comments, then you really are not contributing to the knowledge base. You are just pilfering off someone else's content. When you link to other comments and stories, add a compelling sentence to introduce the topic. If a link has a catch line, people are more likely to click on it. Use graphics to enhance your posts. See Appendix 2, Websites with Pictures for a list of websites that have usable images.

Try customizing the pictures for your posts with a website such as PicMonkey (https://www.picmonkey.com), Canva (https://www.canva.com/create/infographics), or Sumopaint (https://www.sumopaint.com).

If you are involved in more than one interest group, you may not want to send them all the same content. For example, you might be interested in a group for technology and a group for social justice. Tailor the content that you post for each group. For instance, change your hashtags to match the information that you are posting in each group. Not everything that you post for one group will be applicable for others. People will get annoyed if you continue to post things that are irrelevant to them. Posting irrelevant information is a great way to lose connections.

Having a provocative catch line for a post is great. However, you don't need to be controversial all the time. Posting messages to incite difficult conversations on purpose may not foster open dialogue. Before posting something that could incite a flurry of angry posts, consider the consequences related to how you are portraying yourself. Consider the opinion of the people that have the opposite viewpoint. Will your spicy catch line be worth the attention?

If the platform you are using has social media sharing links, use them. Give followers as many ways as possible to expose your ideas to new people. Exposing as many people as possible to your brand will enhance your visibility.

Capitalize on followers. Look at who your followers are following besides you. In addition, consider following your followers. This is a perfect way to help them out and to learn new ideas. Look at their network to see if there are other people that have interests related to your own. People are usually gracious followers when they find someone with something meaningful to say. Plus, following other people is a way to "pay the social connection forward."

Some people build their content organically. When something interesting happens during the day write about it. Perhaps the speaker at a program was exceptional, and they gave a great quote. You can post the quote, a picture of the speaker, and the discussion about the quote. Other people develop a schedule of useful topics. For example, if you are interested in programming, you could develop a calendar of programming ideas that are centered around the months of the year or special events such as Banned Books Week. Regardless of if you decide to post with a schedule or sporadically, you will want to provide engaging content for followers. (Box 7.3).

Depending on the platform, you can post a contact form and allow comments. Read the comments that people leave you. When do you get

BOX 7.3 How do you develop your social media content?

Dr. Jason Alston—My content is mostly a free-for-all. If something pops up in my head, as long as I get to social media in time to put it in a Tweet or put it in a Facebook post, then that is how it is going to get there. I would say that a lot of the things that I share are even things I do not particularly have an interest in, but it may be something to keep my activity going, because I do not want my social media, especially my Twitter to have long periods of time where I do not post something. Sometimes, if I simply see an article that I am even remotely interested in, then that is something that I am likely to Tweet about.

Greg Hardin—My content is usually split between two different things. There is self-marketing and tracking like, here's me and my fellow librarians presenting at a conference or here's us doing some outreach at a table at a student event. Then I include a picture. I also share links and stories. That has a two-fold purpose. I share things that I think are of value and want to be able to get back to or remember. And hopefully other people like it as well.

Dr. Spencer Keralis—I tend to be more of a doctrine of full disclosure kind of person on social media. Where I post my politics, I post my opinions, I post jokes, I post memes and stuff that I think are hilarious, I post music. But I also post my scholarship and the scholarship of people I work with that I respect. I post pop culture stuff. I post events that I'm either involved in, posting about, or think are cool, related to digital humanities and libraries.

kYmberly Keeton—I just wake up and post. I am not out for measurements or what will make people feel good. I did that work by building my website and it took 10 years to build my brand but it is solid.

the most comments? What topic do people usually ask the most questions about? This is the type of content that you want to focus on while searching for similar topics for future posts.

Respond to relevant inquiries. It is just that simple. People do not want to contact posters who are too busy to respond. If you have a comment form, answer the comments. If the comments are appropriate, use them to spark more discussion. While people may post to ask you questions, remember that you can ask your commenters questions about the topic too.

Don't be afraid to ask for comments in your posts. If you don't like the comments that you get, monitor them. You don't have to post everything.

Mix up your content with text, videos, and memes. A meme is a photo or a short video accompanied by humorous text. Memes communicate ideas about social issues. They make fun of behaviors.

Brand yourself with an avatar. Some websites have tools to help you create an avatar or edit a picture that you would like to put on social media sites. Remember that LinkedIn should have a professional picture.

Make yourself personable. You want to share a few details about what makes you unique. However, you don't want all your personal information on social media. While many people endeavor not to mix their personal lives and their professional profiles, sharing a detail or two occasionally can make your brand more likeable. When I suggest sharing something personal, I mean sharing a quick photo stating that you just heard an exceptional speaker at a conference. Your professional profile should not include information about your personal life, such as why you are not with your boyfriend or girlfriend anymore. That is TMI (too much information).

Use consistent graphics for branding. Your website, blog, and other social media pages should have images that are recognizable as you regardless of where you post. Incorporate good quality images. No one wants to see pixelated images online. They are a turnoff and make it seem as if you don't care about your content or are unwilling to put in the effort to improve yourself.

7.1 INFOGRAPHICS

The amount of information that is disseminated continues to grow each year. Information is freely available because of access to the Internet and the amount of time people spend on the Internet each day. Dur (2014) notes that visual communication is powerful because it allows more information to be condensed into a format that can be viewed quickly. When information is presented visually, it can be processed and transferred more quickly than written or audio information. Dur also notes that infographics can be persuasive, can mobilize individuals, and can direct them with calls to action. Presenting information visually in an appealing way can help people to understand the connections between different ideas. Infographics are much more than pictures. Dur states that the purpose of infographics is to tell a story about the content. Infographics are designed to share complex information in an easy- to- understand manner by using a combination of text, illustrations, and maps. Think about it. What can you read quicker, 20 webpages about one topic or one infographic? If you want to convey your topic without information overload, then an infographic is for you.

With a massive amount of content being created and distributed daily on the web, it has become much more challenging to catch and the keep the attention of viewers. Infographics provide a format that utilizes engaging visual that not only appeal to an audience hungry for information, but also aid in the comprehension and retention of that material (Lankow, Crooks, & Ritchie, 2012, p. 12).

The concept of infographics is not new. They have gained more popularity recently. Hamilton's (2014) and Williams' (2013) brief histories of infographics note that the use of graphics or what is now called infographics is not a new phenomenon. According to Williams (2013), cavemen were the first to use drawings to disseminate information on cave walls. Williams defines an infographic as, "any presentation of data that allows the reader to analyze the data using visual comparison" (Williams, 2013, para. 2). However, infographics did not become popular until the 1980s. The launching of USA Today had a great impact on the popularity of infographics in 1982. Graphical representations of information were considered important by the newspaper's editors. Before a story was published, a discussion was held to determine the types of graphics that could be created to enhance it. Infographics were frequently used as standalone elements for stories. Williams (2013) attributes the increase in the popularity of infographics in regional, national, and international new presses to the combination of the expansion in the transmission of information via phone lines, the use of infographics in USA Today, and the ease of desktop publishing for creating statistically accurate illustrated infographics, facilitated by the Apple Macintosh computer.

Highlights from Hamilton and Williams in the development of infographics include the following milestones:

- Cavemen began drawing on cave walls.
- Babylonians used clay tablets in 500 BC.
- Edmond Hailey printed a map showing prevailing winds in 1686. Hailey's map is thought to be the first form of a true infographic (Williams, 2013). Symbols were used to depict trade winds.
- Frances Galton printed the first daily weather map in 1875.
- William Playfair, the founder of graphical statistics, created line graphs, bar charts, pie charts, and circle graphics in 1786. Playfair's work is distinguished because he was one of the first people to plot economic data on a chart.
- Dr. John Snow found the source of the London Cholera Epidemic by plotting cholera deaths on a map in 1854. Snow's work helped to identify the source of the water contamination causing the outbreak.

- The Table of Universal History, a graphic designed to depict the complete history of humans was published in Paris in 1858. It includes a visual of the complete history of humankind, from Adam and Eve to1858.
- Hand-drawn maps were used to show the progress of Civil War battles in newspapers between 1861 and 1865.
- In 1869, Charles Minard charted Napoleon's Russian campaign of 1812. This graph is still considered to be exceptional as it incorporates five types of data: dates, troop strength, locations, weather information, and the direction of movement.
- The assassination of President William McKinley was diagramed in the Chicago Record-Herald in 1901. Eighty years later , the assassination attempt on President Ronald Reagan was illustrated in diagrams.
- Graphics have been used to explain the implications and cost of war beginning with World War I.
- Otto Neurath, the forefather of the pictograms we see today, stressed the importance of visual education and sharing information in a format similar to advertisements in 1925 (Cat, 2017). Neurath developed a picture language that was called Isotype (International System of Typographic Picture Education). Isotypes are simple illustrative representations (icons) of common objects.
- Fritz Khan, a physician and educator, visualized human metabolism as a process of industrial production in 1926 (Rodgers, 2012).
- Fortune magazine started using infographics to illustrate statistics in the 1930s. The introduction of these graphics was thought to be a result of Americans recognizing the usefulness of graphics after the 1929 stock market crash.
- The Lawrence Livermore National Lab published the Chart of Electromagnetic Radiations in 1944.
- Newspapers began to adopt the full-color graphic intensive look for features such as weather maps in 1982.

7.1.1 Types of Infographics

When creating an infographic, an essential step for planning is deciding the type of infographic to create. Venngage blogger McCready (2016) lists nine types of infographics. Can you think of some ideas based on the types of infographics? Let McCready's ideas provide guidance.

7.1.1.1 Statistical

This type of infographic shares the numerical facts that support a topic. This type of infographic is all about presenting data. Numbers are a must. The numbers are combined with graphics, charts, and data to tell a story.

Examples
- An infographic about the number of people that participate in your library programs
- The results of a survey about a program that you created

7.1.1.2 Informational

This type of infographic focuses on conveying text in easy-to-read bullet points. Bullet points and icons are used frequently to convey text quickly. McCready (2016) recommends including headers to highlight concise text.

Examples
- An infographic describing the importance of net neutrality
- A description of the types of book genres

7.1.1.3 Timeline

These infographics focus on the passage of time and the events that occur during a specified time period. Events frequently are placed along a line with various fonts, icons, colors, and headings to emphasize key points along the continuum.

Examples
- A timeline highlighting significant events regarding freedom of speech
- A timeline describing the events and dates of a workshop series you are offering

7.1.1.4 Process

As indicated by the name, the process infographic will illustrate the steps in a process to make it easier to understand. When people finish reading through the steps, they should feel prepared to complete the procedure outlined in the infographic. Like an informational infographic, this info-graphic also will include easy- to- follow bullets with clear headings. Each bullet should contain body text to describe the requirements for the steps. Numbers and/or icons should be an integral part of this type of infographic.

Examples
- The process for booking you for an event
- The process of creating a chart in Excel
- The process for accessing your password protected materials

7.1.1.5 Geographic Infographic

These infographics share information that is specific to locations. They combine maps of locations with facts about them. These visuals look impressive with a combination of graphics, associated text, and bold colors. A legend to distinguish locations along with color-coding for locations increase the readability of these infographics.

Examples
- The locations of Little Free Libraries in a city
- The locations of your upcoming presentations and the topics that will be covered

7.1.1.6 Comparison Infographics

Do you need to compare different types of information? For example, you might compare statistics between locations, the differences between two types of software, or the pros and cons of specific options. Perhaps you would like to compare the facts and highlight the misleading information presented in news stories. A comparison infographic will present the information in a logical format that shows divergent viewpoints. If you are going to create one of these infographics, include a unifying theme to analyze. Use key points and two columns or sections to organize this type of infographic.

Examples
- An infographic showing the differences between student grades at your university for students who do and do not use library services
- A comparison of the Internet speeds in various libraries or schools in a city
- A categorization of the services you offer for different levels of undergraduate courses

7.1.1.7 Hierarchical Infographics

This visualization organizes information into hierarchies. Graphs of the food chain and Bloom's Taxonomy are examples of the information that you would place in this type of infographic. Once again, headers play an important role in these infographics. These headers will have text to describe each level. Coinciding images can provide anchors to support each level. For instance, put a triangle under the graphics along with linear information to denote levels.

Examples
- The information that can be found on each level of a library
- The information that can be found in each category and subcategory on your website

7.1.1.8 Chart-Centric Infographic

These infographics are simple. They are easy to create because programs such as Microsoft Word, Excel, and PowerPoint come with a ton of charts built in. Moreover, programs like Microsoft Excel will help you to choose the best type of chart based on the data that you choose to use. Plug your data into a chart, select some eye-catching colors, create a legend, and you are ready for business. Just place your chart on your page. Frequently, you will find that the chart takes up the entire page.

Examples
- A chart indicating the views found in your most popular blog posts and articles
- A chart with the most popular services used in your library

7.1.1.9 Résumé Infographic

Perhaps you are looking for a position where a regular résumé will not do. Using an infographic is one way to market your unique skills. Although the infographic is not meant to replace your current résumé because some people are traditionalists, it can add some flare to your presentation. Moreover, these infographics are great for sharing on social media. Remember to be professional on the infographic, while communicating your ability to do the job and your skills for completing the job.

Examples of Information to Include
- Include links to flyers and videos that you have created. Include details about your career objectives, experience, education, skills, and contact information.

7.1.1.10 Video Infographic

Do you have a great video that you made about a trending topic? Combine your video (or a great snapshot from your video for print formats) with bullet points containing essential facts and icons. You can also include your regular infographic formats in your video to create a stylish and professional video.

Examples
- A video and statistics advocating for funding for a new program
- Video clips with statistics from your most successful events

7.1.2 Tips for Creating Infographics

- Use complimentary colors. If you are looking for ideas, programs such as Microsoft Word include complimentary color pallets. Many programs for creating infographics have features built in for graphic design. If you are not graphically inclined, there is nothing wrong with using a template.
- Use appropriately sized text. Resize your infographic, review it at 100% on your computer, and print it out. If the text is too small or too big, edit it.
- Use appropriate text fonts. Some fonts are just difficult to read. Try using simple fonts such as Courier, Times New Roman, and Arial to facilitate readability. Fancier fonts can be used sparingly for headers.
- Don't crowd the information. Err on the side of brevity. Infographics do not need long paragraphs. The point of creating them is to communicate information quickly.
- Balance the text and graphics. No one will understand your infographic if it consists of two pictures and three words. Of course, I am exaggerating. Use complimentary graphics that match the context of your infographic. The pictures will enhance the text.
- Use royalty free graphics. You don't want to get in trouble for copyright infringement. Some programs already have built-in graphics that are safe to use. Appendix 2, Websites with Pictures has a list of websites with free photos. Don't forget to review the terms of use before using the photos.
- Support your information with references. Again, you don't want copyright issues. Give people credit for their work.
- Save your infographics using a resolution that is easy to download. You want online readers with slow Internet connections to be able to read your work.

- Develop the infographic so that it is easy to print. Change the settings in the program that you are using to make the infographic a standard paper size.
- Incorporate facts and statistics. They will make your argument more compelling.
- Draw conclusions about the information presented. If you lead the horse to water, help him to drink. Let people know exactly what you are trying to communicate with your infographic. Simply presenting facts and figures is not enough to help everyone draw the conclusion you intended.

7.1.3 Websites and Tools for Creating Infographics

There are a couple of things that you should know about tools for creating infographics. First, some of the tools may be available for free as mobile apps rather than desktop or laptop computer applications. A mobile app is a software program that is created specifically to work on a device such as a phone or a tablet. In addition, it is okay to create your own mash-up using the tools. Plainly stated, some of the tools may not have all the features that you need. If this is the case, put together the resources available in various tools to get what you need. For example, some tools may be easy to use but may charge a fee to use their images. Yet, there are free images online that can be imported into the tool to solve your problem. Also, some tools are made to edit charts or images, while others allow you to insert them, but nothing more. With a little creativity, you can have everything that you need for free.

In addition, knowing when to combine tools, you should also learn to take a screenshot because some tools will not let you download projects unless you upgrade. Some personal computers (PCs) have a function key for printing screen shots. For PCs that do not have a keyboard with a function key and print screen (PrtSc) button, you can take a screen shot by simultaneously clicking on the CTRL key and the PrtSc button at the top of the keyboard. Mac computers have a "grabber" tool that takes screenshots and can be found in the utilities section. Microsoft Word takes screenshots as well. After you take a screenshot in Word, right click to save the screenshot as an image. For detailed instructions about taking screenshots with all types of devices see this website: https://www.take-a-screenshot.org/.

Microsoft programs such as Word, PowerPoint, and Excel are logical choices for creating infographics. However, if you do not have Microsoft, what can you do? This section will share some options for finding the components of a great infographic or finding free programs for designing them.

PicMonkey (www.picmonkey.com) is one of my favorite programs. Once upon a time, it was free to use on your desktop. While you can still design from your desktop or laptop computer, you won't be able to export your designs without a paid membership. That is where the mobile app comes in. The PicMonkey app is still free, and features include the ability to edit pictures and a variety of fonts, backgrounds, and graphics. Users can also apply photo effects and add frames. Sets of pictures that can be used for icons are categorized by themes.

Ribbet (https://www.ribbet.com/) is much like PicMonkey with features such as the ability to edit pictures. Ribbet offers access to backgrounds, fonts, and graphics. Ribbet also includes sets of graphics organized into themes. It is currently free to export your creations in a JPG or a PNG format. Your pictures can also be shared on Facebook, Flickr, and Google Photos, or can be printed. There are minimal ads on the free version.

Stencil (https://getstencil.com) has over a million royalty free images to use for the projects that you are passionate about. This online editing program also includes icons and quotes to make projects easier. Using some images and the templates requires a membership. The best part is that a free account will allow you to use up to 10 images a month. Projects can be saved and shared online.

Canva (www.canva.com) is another online site for editing photos. You can get started for free and upgrade to access premium features. Upload your own images to save money. Canva includes templates for generating quick projects. Canva provides access to photos, icons, and layouts for graphic design. Canva is available to use with computers or in an app. Finished products can be shared online and downloaded in PDF, PNG, and JPG formats.

Google Drive (https://drive.google.com) is much like Microsoft Word, PowerPoint, and Excel. You can also use Google Forms to create surveys for your online interactive infographics. This is a free cloud-based alternative. Most of the same features are available and Google Drive makes it easy to incorporate graphics from online. The key is to make sure that you give credit to the graphics and search for images with the correct copyright license. If you have a Google account, you already have Google Drive.

Easel.ly (https://www.easel.ly) is a cloud-based website for creating infographics. Users can sign up for a free account that includes images, photos, charts, fonts, templates, and automatic public access to their work. A premium account is needed to access more features and to keep infographics private. Downloads of work are available in a JPEG format.

Infogram (https://infogram.com/) is another online tool for creating infographics, charts, and reports. The free basic account includes interactive charts, maps, and the ability to publish up to 10 projects online with up to three pages per project. Users can also import data for their projects. An account must be upgraded to activate the privacy settings. Popular project types include infographics, reports, Facebook posts, charts, and maps. Other types of projects include email headers and posts for LinkedIn, Twitter, Instagram, and Pinterest.

Venngage (https://venngage.com) lets you work with a drag-and-drop interface to create infographics. Data from Google Drive Spreadsheets can be imported easily into infographics. Interactive features include polls, forms, and YouTube videos. Users have access to charts, maps, pictographs, frames, images, and backgrounds. However, the free account will allow you to create five infographics only. They must be made publicly available, unless you upgrade to a premium account.

Visme (https://www.visme.co/) is an infographic maker that allows you to create three projects with a free basic account. The tool includes 100 MB of storage and limited templates, charts, and widgets. Projects can be downloaded and are available in a JPG or a PNG format. Projects published on the basic plan are made public.

Vizualize.me (http://vizualize.me/) turns résumés into infographics for free. You can connect a LinkedIn profile to build your profile quickly, or you can type in each element individually. After you add your information, including work experience, education, links, skills, interests, languages, awards, honors, and stats, you can customize the infographic with themes, colors, fonts, and a background. You can also get your own customized Vizualize.me link.

Google Charts (https://developers.google.com/chart/) is great for visualizing data on a website. From simple pie graphs and bar graphs to complex tree maps, you can create just about any type of chart that you can think of. Then you can use the code to embed the chart into your website. Each chart is customizable to fit your website's design. Remember to follow the QuickStart guide to prepare your website. If you find Google Charts daunting, simply use the chart tools inside of

Google's word processor (drive.google.com). You will be able to design a chart without the HTML to place inside of your website's code.

Piktochart (https://piktochart.com/) offers a free account with unlimited infographics. When using the free account, you can download your infographics in a PNG format or share them using a link. There are also social media sharing options and thousands of icons and images to accentuate your creativity. Additional features include text frames, a variety of fonts, charts, the ability to insert YouTube and Vimeo videos, and maps. You can upload JPG, PNG, GIF, and SVG images to your documents. The basic account offers 40 MB of free storage for images. You can also use the shapes and icons, lines, photos, and photo frames for free. An added benefit is that Piktochart makes infographics for online use, presentations slides, and printable formats. Each format has free templates.

Online Chart Tool (https://www.onlinecharttool.com) uses a step-by-step process for designing charts. You do not have to log into this resource to use it. Twelve types of chart formats are available with the ability to customize the chart elements with fonts and colors. When information is entered for each step, users will find a "next" button to access the next step. Charts can be saved in multiple formats. Generated charts and applicable data can be downloaded in high resolution, SVG, PNG, JPG, PDF, and CSV formats. This includes the option to generate HTML code or a link. Charts can also be saved and edited later.

WordClouds.com (http://www.wordclouds.com) is a free word cloud generator that can be used to create graphics for your website. A login is not required. There is a wizard to help you edit your project. After putting in the words by pasting or uploading them, you can change the shape, size, color themes, and font of your creation. Moreover, a background from your computer can be uploaded. Images can be saved as a PDF, JPG, or PNG. They can also be shared on Google Plus, Facebook, or Twitter. According to the "Frequently Asked Questions," you are free to use the images any way that you want to, even commercially. Of course, the website always appreciates credit, but it is not required.

ToonyTool.com (https://www.toonytool.com/) is an online tool for creating cartoons and comics. The interface is simple. You start by choosing a background or uploading your own. Next, you can insert characters on your own and then add the text bubbles and props. The final project can be turned into a meme. (A meme is an image, text, or video that can be spread throughout the Internet to deliver a message. The message can be funny, satirical, and/ or philosophical.)

Diagram Editor (https://www.diagrameditor.com/) is an online tool designed to create diagrams quickly. The tool does not require a log in and comes with several types of shapes built in. Users can easily designate the relationships between diagram elements, set the size of the page, insert shapes and icons, and change fonts. Images can be incorporated into charts. Diagram Editor accepts imports from Google Drive, Dropbox, OneDrive, URLS, and your browser. Final products can be exported in PNG, JPEG, SVG, PDF, HTML, VSDZ, and XML formats. They can also be embedded or published as a link.

Wordle (www.wordle.net) is another word cloud generator. Words that appear more frequently in the text are written larger. Text is pasted into a large textbox to create the word cloud. There is nothing to download. Word clouds can be edited with different fonts, layouts, and color schemes. Please note that Java is required to use this tool. While Wordle will give you code to embed the word cloud, some people state that the image is too small. You can also get a large image by taking a screen shot and saving the image.

7.1.4 Including Research Results and Statistics in Infographics

There are a variety of places to find facts and statistics to incorporate into your infographics. Remember that it is always important to cite any idea that is not your own. Perhaps you have a topic that you are passionate about. The first way to generate statistics for your infographics is to conduct your own research. Keep in mind that research should follow proper protocols as outlined by your institution's Human Subjects Board. Learn more about these protocols by consulting with your institution's Human Subjects Board and by taking a free class offered by the National Institutes of Health (https://phrp.nihtraining.com/users/login.php). Then complete all necessary applications.

Sometimes you may want to create an infographic about the topic without gathering your own data. A logical way to achieve your goal is to look at current research about the topic and to gather all foundational articles related to the topic as well. Statistics can also be obtained by citing original research articles. For example, you know that danah boyd and Nicole Ellison are experts who publish about social networking sites. You also know that Jean Twenge has recently published an article about youth and social networking. Gather the information that you need about the topic and cite it in your own infographic. In this way, you are educating yourself about current research and establishing yourself as an expert.

7.1.5 Last Thoughts on Infographics

In conclusion, infographics are an excellent way to market your skills and share information about topics that you want to advocate for. However, while creating, make sure that the information that you are sharing is unique by adding your own twist to the concepts presented. Tell your readers why they need to know about the topic. When you are creating your infographic, be sure that you are capturing the most important points. An infographic is the same as a PowerPoint in many aspects. I imagine you have seen the *Death by PowerPoint* video by Phillips (2014) in which he asserts that too much text is a no-no.

Citing your sources of information is a must. Double-check the information and make sure that it is correct. Use a reliable source for your statistics. (See Appendix 1, Sources for Data and Statistics, for a list of statistic sources.) You can also use peer reviewed and professional journals to get the latest information about your topic. Hypothetically, these sources have been checked by professionals before they were published, and the review process adds a layer of protection to your own work.

Cite with a consistent style, as there are many to choose from. Consult a website like the Citation Machine (www.citationmachine.net) to create consistent citations. If you have access to RefWorks (www.refworks.com) through your university, it is also a great option that saves, formats, and organizes your sources. RefWorks creates a personal database of your references. Microsoft Word includes capabilities for creating citations and can be integrated with RefWorks. Google Scholar creates citations as well. Endnote is another software for creating your own reference database. As of January 2018, a basic Endnote account is free (http://endnote.com/product-details/basic). Just remember that regardless of the type of citation engine or software you use to create a database, you need to enter the information correctly and check the format after the software makes a suggestion for the citation.

7.2 CHAPTER CHALLENGES

1. Attend a Twitter chat to determine the most frequently asked questions about your topic. Look for the responses for those questions and turn them into an infographic. Post the infographic online.
2. Look at some of the resources in Appendix 1, Sources for Data and Statistics. Think of a research question related to your personal brand

and find statistics that you can share about the topic in a presentation posted on YouTube.

3. Analyze your social media likes and responses from your followers. What days and times are the most active for you? Create a schedule based on those days and times.

REFERENCES

Cat, J. (2017). Otto Neurath. In: Zalta EN, editor. *The Stanford Encyclopedia of Philosophy (Winter 2017 Edition)*. Retrieved from <https://plato.stanford.edu/archives/win2017/entries/neurath/> (accessed 2017.12.27).

Dur, B. I. U. (2014). Data visualization and infographics in visual communication design education at the age of information. *Journal of Arts and Humanities, 3*(5), 39—50. Retrieved from <http://theartsjournal.org/index.php/site/article/view/460/267> (accessed 2017.12.27).

Hamilton, K. (2014). *A brief history of information graphics/infographics.* Retrieved from (https://www.slideshare.net/kehamilt/a-brief-history-of-information-graphicsinfographics) (accessed 2017.12.27).

Lankow, J., Crooks, R., & Ritchie, J. (2012). *Infographics: the power of visual storytelling.* Hoboken, NJ: Wiley.

McCready, R. (2016). *The top 9 infographic template types.* Retrieved from (https://venngage.com/blog/9-types-of-infographic-template/) (accessed 2017.12.27).

Phillips, D.J.P. (2014). *Death by PowerPoint.* Retrieved from (https://youtu.be/Iwpi1Lm6dFo) (accessed 2017.12.27).

Rodgers, S. (2012). *Infographics old and new: top data visualisations, in pictures.* Retrieved from (http://www.theguardian.com/news/datablog/2012/mar/16/infographics-data-visualisation-history) (accessed 2017.12.27).

Williams, M. (2013). Informational graphics. In Margaret A. Blanchard (Ed.), *History of the mass media in the United States: An encyclopedia.* New York, NY: Routledge.

CHAPTER 8

Social Media Safety and Privacy

Figure 8.1 Privacy concept photo.

8.1 PRIVACY AND SOCIAL MEDIA

What does privacy on a social media website really mean? Many social media platforms and tools are offered for free. However, they must be used with caution. What do you agree to when you use social media? Are you selling your privacy and personal information? In April 2017, a controversy unfolded when Unroll.me's co-founder wrote a blunt email about the company selling user information. Unroll.me is a service that helps users to unsubscribe to subscription emails instantly. The website's "Terms & Conditions" page includes the following information under the "Information About You and Your Visits to the Website" section.

> All information we collect on this Website is subject to our Privacy Notice. By using the Website, you consent to all actions taken by us with respect to your information in compliance with the Privacy Policy. You represent and warrant that all data provided by you is accurate (Unroll.me, 2017b, para. 9).

The Privacy Policy further states that under the "Our Collection and use of Non-Personal Information" section that,

> We may collect, use, transfer, sell, and disclose non-personal information for any purpose. For example, when you use our services, we may collect data from and about the "commercial electronic mail messages" and "transactional or relationship messages" (as such terms are defined in the CAN-SPAM

Act (15 U.S.C. 7702 et. seq.) that are sent to your email accounts … We may disclose, distribute, transfer, and sell such messages and the data that we collect from or in connection with such messages; provided, however, if we do disclose such messages or data, all personal information contained in such messages will be removed prior to any such disclosure. (Unroll.me, 2017a, para. 3)

When the company collects data and aggregates it, it no longer considers the data to be private. It is also stated that Unroll.me collects personal and nonpersonal information when customers visit the website. This information can include IP addresses and telephone numbers (Unroll.me, 2017a).

The data collected by Unroll.me is not unique. As noted by the cofounder of Unenroll.me, collecting, aggregating, and selling data collected through their websites is one way for companies offering free services to generate money (Digg Blog, 2017). Each time a potential user signs up for a service, they agree to the policies of the company. Like Unroll.me, many companies use cookies, log files, information shared on their websites, and choices made on websites to build profiles for customers. For example, Facebook collected personal data from millions of users. The data was exploited by the firm Cambridge Analytica to build models for psychographic messaging targeting voters. This messaging was used to sway 2016 election results in the United States (Rosenberg, Confessore, & Cadwalladr, 2018). Buyer beware (Fig. 8.2).

8.2 PROTECTING YOUR PRIVACY

Have you searched for yourself online lately? Have you looked at the pictures that are associated with your name? Is your phone number, address, and email address plastered on websites such as Spokeo? What comments are people writing about you? Being online and using social media is not something that is just for fun. It is a serious activity that warrants constant monitoring. In fact, there are tools and companies such as RemoveYourName (https://www.removeyourname.com), ReputationDefender (https://www.reputationdefender.com), Reputation Management Consultants (https://www.reputationmanagementconsultants.com), and Rankur (https://rankur.com/) that specialize in monitoring and managing online reputations. One must be aware of their image at all times and understand that a digital footprint is being left online. Your digital footprint is the trail of information that you leave about yourself online. Each website that is joined or visited offers a potential breach of your reputation and online security.

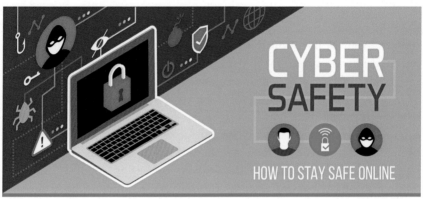

Figure 8.2 Online safety infographic.

You can take measures to protect your privacy on social media. Social media networks collect a variety of details about you when you sign up for services. You do not want this information to be accessible to the wrong people. In its most basic form, being secure online begins with not sharing too much. One should never share passwords, especially via email.

Another fundamental way to protect your privacy is to use the tools that social media platforms have to offer. Do not accept the default settings for social media platforms. Investigate your options. If there are extra protocols that can be enacted, accept them. For example, Twitter has a basic login protocol; then it allows you to set up login verification. Twitter also has password reset verification that requires a phone number and email before resetting a password. Furthermore, there are other options that you can use for help with your passwords.

1. Create long passwords. Simple words will make your password easier to guess. Try using the first letters of a sentence in your favorite song or book.
2. Do not use your name, your company's name, a dictionary word, or the name of a significant place, person, or pet in your passwords. If you tell everyone on social media that you love your dog Fluffy, then you put Fluffy's name in all your passwords, you are leaving yourself open to attacks.
3. Include at least one number that is not related to a recognizable date in your life.
4. Consider using a security manager software to help keep your passwords private. Henry (2017) suggests the following programs: LastPass, Dashlane, KeePass, 1Password, and Roboform.
5. Use at least one character (!@#$%^&*) in your passwords.
6. Use at least one randomly placed uppercase and lowercase letter in passwords.
7. Use a different password for each website. If you use the same password for multiple social media sites and get hacked one time, you are likely to get hacked on the rest of the websites.
8. Frequently change your passwords. Change to a new password every month or so.

8.3 SOCIAL MEDIA MISTAKES

Blue (2015) points out several mistakes that people make with social media. For instance, people frequently check in on social media to tell others where they are attending a conference or eating out. If you live in New York City and you have your home location posted on your account, and you tell everyone that you are in San Francisco for a conference, clearly you are not at home. Sharing your whereabouts leaves you open to having your house robbed, especially if you have pictures posted online that tell the location of your home. Some apps such as Facebook will tag your photos with your location? In addition, you want to check to see if your mobile apps are "listening" or "watching" your daily activities. As such, it is a good practice to cover your webcam. You need to turn these features off in the settings.

Blue also notes that you should be careful about where you are signing into your social media apps. Public networks at airports and hotels can leave you open to getting viruses that steal your information. Furthermore, if you sign into a public computer or device, you risk leaving your information open after you believe you have signed off. If you trust the computer or device that does not belong to you, be sure that you shut it down after you get off. Consider that you might be inadvertently sharing your information on a device that has a screen recording or keystroke recording app enabled. Be careful about the networks and devices you use.

While using one email address is convenient, consider having multiple addresses for your online accounts. Blue suggests that the emails from multiple accounts can be forwarded to your preferred account. Similarly, get a VoIP (Voice over Internet Protocol) phone number for Internet use. The messages for these accounts can be forwarded as well.

Blue (2015, p. 23) further encourages readers to understand that there are just some details about life that should not be shared online. These details include:

- Your family member names and profiles
- Your social security and ID numbers
- Personal addresses
- The location and date of where you were born
- Financial information such as bank account and credit card numbers
- Information that you typically use to answer password questions

Moreover, with any social media site, it is imperative to be selective about whom you befriend. In LinkedIn, one answers invitations or sends invitations to get new contacts. Contacts are the equivalent of what is referred to as friends on Facebook or followers on Twitter. Adding individuals to your network without adequately checking them can seem harmless. Nonetheless, hackers' use of fake profiles on LinkedIn has been brought to the forefront in the news (BBC News, 2015).

Hackers set up fake profiles by populating them with information and using stock photos of men and women online. Roth (2017, para. 2) explains the danger of adding a fake LinkedIn profile to your network.

Connecting with a scam or fake profile on LinkedIn can give the scammer access to powerful data about you. If you have it enabled, LinkedIn has your contact email address available to connections from your profile page. It also lets connections see detailed information about your history, company and professional contacts that could be used to craft detailed and believable phishing and other scams against you.

Before adding someone to your network, investigate them. Even individuals that are connected to other people in your network could be fake. Take the time to examine their profiles to investigate their employment and educational history. Can you find the person elsewhere online? For example, if they list an employer, does the employer acknowledge them in the contact information displayed online. Do they have a page that is on the employer's website? Does the information that they post on LinkedIn look legitimate? Are you able to verify that they have presented at a conference and posted the presentation online? Have they published in a journal, association page, or in a magazine? These are all indicators that the person is legitimate.

Many hackers are posing as recruiters. Moreover, details of the fake accounts are duplicated from successful professionals to make them seem authentic. Many of them can establish a large number of contacts. Then they request personal information from unsuspecting victims that are eager to find a job (Sordyl, 2017). When the victim takes the bait, the fake recruiter will ask for personal information to steal their identities.

The profile of Mia Ash on LinkedIn is an example of how a fake profile can trick unsuspecting networkers (Palmer, 2017). The profile was set up to infiltrate organizations in the financial, oil, and technology sectors with Trojan malware. The Mia Ash profile portrayed a woman that worked as a photographer in London. Starting in April 2016, the profile amassed 500 (Palmer, 2017) connections and many more on Facebook.

The profile, controlled by hackers, began by connecting with photographers to look trustworthy. Next, it started connecting with powerful men in various target organizations. The profile was active and frequently received comments on photos from its targets. After communicating on LinkedIn, the conversations eventually gravitated to email. Then the Ash profile sent files that needed to be opened at work to function properly (Palmer, 2017). The files contained a Trojan virus to give hackers access to the victims' organizational network. Though the Mia Ash profile was noticed, the hacking group is still active and engineering attacks.

> ## BOX 8.1 How do you share on social media without giving too much information?
>
> *Kelly Hoppe—I just know that coming from a school setting, it was just drilled into me over the course of my career and also as a personal belief, to be careful about what you say, because it can come back to you. And it's also a reflection of you in your job. I don't want to come across negative. I want people to follow me because they enjoy what I'm Tweeting, that they find humor in some of the things that I Tweet, and they're interested in creative things that we're doing in our library.*
>
> *Ayla Stein—I have very strong opinions, and I do not mind sharing them. I also enjoy debating with people, as long as it doesn't devolve into attacks. Once it is an attack, I block you, because once the conversation has sunk to that level, there's no point in continuing.*

The bottom line is that you need to do your due diligence when using social networks to make professional connections. Recruiters should only ask you for information through official websites designated by their companies. Check the pages to ensure that they are legitimate, instead of being a duplicate of a legitimate website. Make a phone call to check the legitimacy of the company before sharing your personal information. Use a PO box on your resume.

Other ways to check the legitimacy of a profile include completing a reverse image search on Google by dragging and dropping the profile image into Google images or pasting profile information into Google (Roth, 2017). From there, you can begin to verify the details of the account. Roth (2017) also notes that fake LinkedIn profiles frequently have spelling errors, professional associations to influential people that are too good to be true, and work histories that do not make sense. Roth notes that a person that graduated from a prestigious university is not likely to settle for working as a secretary right after graduating from college. If a person's profile does not make sense, you do not need to associate with them. If you use these steps and find that a person is not legitimate, end the relationship immediately and report their suspicious activity to the social media network (Box 8.1).

8.4 RECOGNIZING SCAMS

Van Susteren (2017, p. 268–269) asserts that many online scams are adaptions of age-old schemes to blackmail and manipulate people. Being able to recognize them can help you to avoid them. Some of the tactics include:

Clickjacking: Using an attention-grabbing headline on an ad or article to encourage people to click on them. After people click on the item, a malicious computer code will tell the social media website that a person has liked the content and signify that the site should forward it to the news feeds of friends. This activity is prominent on Facebook. If you hover over these types of ads or articles, the links will not begin with https. Check links before clicking on them.

Doxing: The practice of sharing private details about a person on the Internet. These details often include information linked to court records which can be embarrassing. Doxing occurs when people are being hateful or want to blackmail another person. Avoid sharing personal information online and face-to-face.

Pharming or phishing: The practice of sending fake emails and messages that trick people into telling their personal information or sending money for various purposes. Phishing emails will often encourage you to click on a link to complete a task like updating an account. They will include requests such as sending your bank account or credit card numbers and passwords. When you click on the link or send information, your account or computer will be taken over. Don't click on emails from strange people and verify links and company names by searching for them online. You can always call to ask questions as well. While there is no foolproof way to know if a message is phishing, if it does not feel right, do not respond.

Security Alarms: Occur when your computer sends you a message that your browser has been hacked. Do not click on these messages. Do not pay for the software offered through these messages. Nor should you talk to anyone associated with a service on one of these messages. It is best to use your own malware software.

8.5 KNOWING WHEN YOU HAVE BEEN HACKED

There are signs that indicate when you have been hacked. These signs include not being able to access your accounts, finding that you do not have as many friends as you had, and finding friends that you would not normally associate with on social media networks. Your accounts may display posts that you have not made. There could be strange emails in your inbox or being sent from your account.

If you find that you have been hacked, here are some measures that you can take. Call your credit card companies to change your cards. Let your bank know that you were a victim of identity theft and asked them to refund and stop erroneous transactions. Change all of your passwords. Check your computer to determine if malware is installed. If your email has been used to send messages, warn your contacts.

In conclusion, the best way to protect yourself online and when you are using social media is to be overly cautious. There is a ton of information stored on your phone, computer, or tablet. To prevent people from stealing this information, enable remote wiping software to erase your information just in case the device is stolen. Putting a tracking mechanism or locator on your devices is also helpful for detecting them. Furthermore, consider using the private browsing setting when you are searching the Internet.

When considering privacy, less information posted online is better. Depending on the social network, the default for posting information may not be private. You do not want to tell people personal details that can be used to hurt you. Always think about what you are doing and the impact that it can have on your life. No one should be able to determine your daily routine by watching you online. Innocently telling someone on social media that you are home alone or on your way to your favorite restaurant can have devastating consequences. Don't broadcast everything about your life. Refrain from making recordings of your surroundings that can help malicious individuals map out your work and living environments. Turn the location indicators off on social media so that they are not tracking you. Think before you act.

8.6 CHAPTER CHALLENGES

1. Search for yourself on the Internet. What did you find? If you find invasive or incorrect information posted online by a company, contact them to learn about their opt-out procedure.
2. Look at your social media profiles without being logged in. Determine if you are sharing personal information such as your date of birth, phone number, and address. Edit your profiles accordingly.

REFERENCES

BBC News. (2015). *Fake LinkedIn profiles used by hackers*. Retrieved from (http://www.bbc.com/news/technology-34994858) (accessed 17.09.15).

Blue, V. (2015). *The smart girl's guide to privacy: Practical tips for staying safe online*. San Francisco, CA: No Starch Press.

Digg Blog. (2017). *Unroll.me's cofounder responds to criticism with an exceptionally blunt blog post*. Retrieved from ⟨http://digg.com/2017/unroll-me-uber-controversy⟩ (accessed 17.09.15).

Henry, A. (2017). *The five best password managers*. ⟨https://lifehacker.com/5529133/five-best-password-managers⟩ (accessed 17.09.15).

Palmer, D. (2017). *How these fake Facebook and LinkedIn profiles tricked people into friending state-backed hackers*. Retrieved from ⟨http://www.zdnet.com/article/how-these-fake-facebook-and-linkedin-profiles-tricked-people-into-friending-state-backed-hackers/⟩ (accessed 17.09.15).

Rosenberg, M., Confessore, N., & Cadwalladr, C. (2018). How Trump consultants exploited the Facebook data of millions. Retrieved from < https://www.nytimes.com/2018/03/17/us/politics/cambridge-analytica-trump-campaign.html > (accessed 18.05.28).

Roth, C. (2017). *How to keep yourself safe from fake LinkedIn profiles*. Retrieved from ⟨https://www.entrepreneur.com/article/287398⟩ (accessed 17.09.15).

Sordyl, M. (2017). Fake recruiter scams and how to avoid them. Retrieved from < https://www.linkedin.com/pulse/fake-recruiter-scams-how-avoid-them-mathew-sordyl// > (accessed 18.05.28).

Unroll.me (2017a). *Privacy policy*. Retrieved from ⟨https://unroll.me/legal/privacy/⟩ (accessed 17.09.15).

Unroll.me. (2017b). *Terms and conditions*. Retrieved from ⟨https://unroll.me/legal/terms/⟩ (accessed 17.09.15).

Van Susteren, G. (2017). *Everything you need to know about social media: Without having to call a kid*. New York, NY: Simon & Schuster Paperbacks.

CHAPTER 9

Blogging

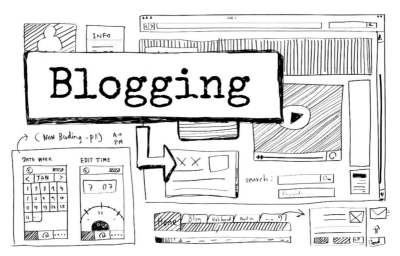

Figure 9.1 Blogging clip art.

9.1 GETTING STARTED WITH WORDPRESS

According to Burns (2017), free blogging software was released by Pitas and Blogger in 1999. This software facilitated the use of blogs because of the easy interfaces. While Pitas is no longer in existence, Blogger is still available today. Google purchased it in the early 2000s. Other popular blogging websites include Tumblr, Storify, EduBlogs, LinkedIn, and Medium. WordPress is currently the most used blogging platform.

In the United States, it was estimated that in the spring of 2017, 28.79 million people read or contributed to blogs on computers within a 30-day period (Nielsen Scarborough, 2017). These are over 28 million individuals that are potential viewers for your materials online. A blog can give you a resource for bringing together all your social media network posts and your resume. This chapter will provide some brief tips for starting a blog with WordPress.

Growing Your Library Career with Social Media
DOI: https://doi.org/10.1016/B978-0-08-102411-9.00009-1

Getting started with WordPress.com is easy. Note there is a difference between Wordpress.org and Wordpress.com. For Wordpress.org, you will need to install the software and look for your hosting. With Wordpress.com, everything is included in the price. You can choose between several levels of accounts. There is a free account with a domain for your blog that includes your username on Wordpress.com. Getting started with the free WordPress domain is an excellent way to learn about WordPress before investing money. Otherwise, you can choose to purchase your own domain to enhance your online professional presence.

WordPress will initiate a series of questions to set up your account. Take special care with setting up your domain. The ideal domain name is something that gives a clear indication of what your blog is about, is catchy, unique, and easy to remember. Once you have some options shortlisted, double-check for availability. One domain name can't be allocated to more than one blog or website. On the contrary, domain names can be similar. Search the Internet to see if there is a comparable domain. Furthermore, WordPress will indicate if a prospective domain is available.

After you finish answering the questions and verifying your account, you will be taken to the dashboard which WordPress refers to as the My Site menu. As you change the settings on your account, WordPress will present various pop-ups for guidance.

You can change your site theme or appearance when you click on the Customize button in the menu. WordPress has hundreds of themes that can be used. A lot of them are free. Keep in mind that a responsive layout will adjust to multiple devices allowing individuals on tablets, computers, and phones to read your content. WordPress will provide tips for setting up each theme when you click on them.

9.2 STATS

The Stats link is helpful for determining how many people are viewing your content, the number of likes that you have, and comments. WordPress will disclose the countries your visits originate from, the posts and pages that are popular, the search terms that are being used to access your blog, and the videos that are the most popular. If another page is referring viewers to your blog, you will see that information too.

9.3 SETTINGS

The menu includes a Settings link. Use this link to customize and verify the settings for your blog. There are several components on the Settings page. In fact, there are four tabs that can be selected.

9.3.1 General Settings

The first tab in the Settings link is the General tab. You can change the Site Title on the General tab in Settings. The Site Title is different from your domain name. The Site Title is a heading that will appear at the top of your page. The Site Tag Line provides a brief description of the site.

The Site Address can be changed if you are using a free WordPress domain. You can also use a custom domain through WordPress or map a domain that you have purchased elsewhere on your website. If you buy a domain when you set up the website, it will show in the Site Address area.

Next, choose your language and your time zone. You can also decide if your website will be public for everyone to see, hidden and not indexed by search engines, or private. If the site is private, it will only be visible to people that you approve of seeing it.

There is another area for the Footer Credit. The Footer Credit cannot be removed unless the account is a business account. Otherwise, there are options to choose from such as "Blog with WordPress" and "Powered by WordPress."

There is a Site Tools section that enables users to:
- Change the site address
- Import content from another WordPress or Medium site
- Export content from the current site
- Delete content to wipe the site clean
- Delete the site permanently

9.3.2 Writing Settings

The Writing tab will tell you how many categories and tags are associated with posts. New tags and categories can be developed using this page or when posts are written.

The Composing section asks if you would like to have a confirmation before publishing a post. It also sets the default post format and the date and time format for posts.

The Content Types section settings determine how many blog posts are displayed per page. The number of testimonials per page and the number of portfolio projects are displayed per page. WordPress allows users to add a separate portfolio to their website. For instance, if you have pictures of you presenting at a conference, you might want to display them in a collection. If your selected theme format does not include a portfolio option, the code can be inserted to add one. Each portfolio will have a separate name. They can be categorized by types or tags.

WordPress blogs can have RSS feeds. Feeds are created automatically by WordPress. Posts that have been marked private are not incorporated into feeds. The Feed Settings section lets you determine how many posts to add into feeds and if posts will be limited to an excerpt.

Theme Enhancements control whether readers of your blog will have a continuous stream of posts or will have to click a button to load more posts.

Finally, Press This is an app that will run in your browser. When you find content that you like, you can "grab" it for your blog by clicking on the app icon. You can use text, images, and videos from other content online in your posts and add comments about the content.

9.3.3 Discussion Settings

These settings are for monitoring reactions to your commentary. There are Default Article Settings that will notify other blogs linked to articles posted on your website, notify you when there are links from other blogs, and allow people to comment on your posts.

The Comments section covers the requirements for posting to your blog. For example, will readers be required to share a name and email address before posting to your blog? You can control settings such as when commenting closes, how many threads can be nested within comments, and if readers are required to register before commenting on posts.

You can use the Email Me Whenever section to determine when WordPress will send notifications about your blog. These notifications include:

- When someone makes a comment
- When a comment needs to be moderated
- When someone likes a post
- When your post is reblogged
- When someone follows your blog

The last couple of sections of the Discussion Settings page provide settings for blacklisting commenters by adding their IP address to a list, deciding how many hyperlinks are required before a comment is held for moderation, and if comments must be manually approved.

9.3.4 Traffic Settings

WordPress has tools to optimize traffic located on the Traffic settings tab. Some of these tools (Google Analytics and Search Engine Optimization) will not be available unless you have upgraded to the business plan. You can, however, drive traffic to other posts by telling WordPress to show content related to other posts. Furthermore, WordPress can improve how mobile pages load for quicker access. Your sitemap will automatically be indexed by search engines. You can verify your site, so that it is indexed by search engines such as Google, Bing, Pinterest, and Yandex. WordPress provides code and directions for each blog.

9.4 WRITING A NEW POST

Blogging is all about sharing content. Of course, you may decide to set your blog to look like a website instead of a blog, but you will still need to post. To write a new post, go to the top of the page and click on the Write button. You can use the Visual or HTML view. The Visual view is like a WYSIWYG (what you see is what you get). The Visual view is useful if you do not know HTML. The HTML view is always handy if you know HTML and desire precise results. For instance, sometimes WordPress will add extra space between lines. It is difficult to eliminate the space unless you know how to manipulate HTML code.

Writing a blog post with WordPress is much like working with a word processor like Microsoft Word. The Add button enables you to include media such as pictures and videos. You can feature a payment button, a contact form, and vetted images from a free photo library. Moreover, you can display pictures from your Google account after you have connected it.

The Paragraph button has a drop-down menu with features for formatting text in a paragraph. You can use headings or simply use the paragraph setting. You can also use preformatted text. Then there are the icons that you typically see in a word processor. If you are having difficulty in determining their purpose, hover over them for a moment, and WordPress will tell you what they mean.

Copying and pasting text from your word processor is an easy way to write a post. After you have entered the title and commentary, there will be options to preview or publish the post. There are also several links in a menu on the right side of the page. Under the Status button, you can decide when to publish a post and if the post will be public. The post can also be "stuck" to the front page of your blog.

There is a Categories & Tags section. By default, new posts will be categorized as "Uncategorized" until tags and categories have been assigned. Create new categories and add tags as needed.

You can set a featured image for a blog post. The featured image will be shown when subscribers get an alert about a newly published blog post.

The Sharing section will send your post to social media. If you have not connected any social media services, you can do that here. Share buttons can be selected to appear under posts.

The More Options section will let you write an excerpt of your post, put in your current location, allow comments from readers, and enable pingbacks and trackbacks from other blogs.

9.5 CONCLUSION

In conclusion, if you do not currently have a blog, you might want to get one for displaying your social media content and posting content to social media from one place. Set a schedule that is easy for you to maintain. Alternatively, WordPress will let you set up a blog that looks like a website instead of a traditional blog. Then frequent posts do not need to be made. Consider that having a blog can give you a way to market and sell content online. Blogs are an excellent venue for advertising classes you are teaching and presentations that you are making. If you need ideas for your blog, consider reading some of the blogs in Appendix 6, Blogs for Librarians.

9.6 CHAPTER CHALLENGES

1. WordPress is a convenient platform for blogging. However, it is not the only option available. Take some time to look at the features of other platforms such as Tumblr, Storify, EduBlogs, LinkedIn, and Medium. Compare the pricing features and templates available. Which platform is the best for your needs?

2. Look at some of the blogs in Appendix 6, Blogs for Librarians. What are the trending topics? Based on the topics that you find, which niche relative to your skills is not covered?

REFERENCES

Burns, K. S. (2017). *Social media: A reference handbook*. Santa Barbara, CA: ABC-CLIO.
Nielsen Scarborough. (2017). Number of Internet users who engaged with blogs on computer within the last month in the United States from autumn 2013 to spring 2017 (in millions). In: *Statista—The statistics portal*. Retrieved from ⟨https://libproxy.library.unt.edu:9076/statistics/479180/internet-users-who-engaged-with-blogs-on-computer-within-the-last-month-usa/⟩ (accessed 18.01.15).

CHAPTER 10

Bringing It All Together

Figure 10.1 Social network computer.

10.1 INTRODUCTION

As this book closes, I will admit that it only scratches the surface of what is available in the social media sphere for personal branding and professional development. There are many technologies that are not included. However, I hope that you will take the time to review the list of tools available in Appendix 4, Social Media Networks and Tools. In addition, Table 10.1 contains resources for learning more about social media. There are some honorable mentions that you should be aware of:

- Google + is like Facebook in that it is used for connecting families and friends.
- Snapchat is emerging as a way to share moments on video.

Growing Your Library Career with Social Media
DOI: https://doi.org/10.1016/B978-0-08-102411-9.00010-8
147

Table 10.1 Websites that Teach About Social Media

eMarketing Institute	https://www.emarketinginstitute.org/free-courses/
GCFLearnFree.org	https://www.gcflearnfree.org/topics/socialmedia/
Hootsuite Academy	https://education.hootsuite.com/
Moz	https://moz.com/beginners-guide-to-social-media
Social Fresh	https://www.socialfresh.com/
Social Media Training	http://socialmediatraining.com/social-media-training/

- Instagram is great for sharing photos and brief commentary about them.
- Tumblr is another microblogging and social networking website to explore.

If you would like to go beyond social media to maintaining your own websites, you will have to find hosting or use a service that includes hosting. Many people use the services offered by GoDaddy (https://www.godaddy.com) because one can get a domain name and use GoDaddy's website builder to have a website up and going in an hour. If you don't have good website development skills, About.me offers a quick way to create a basic website for highlighting your accomplishments and linking together your social media accounts. In addition, Weebly (https://www.weebly.com/) and Wix (https://www.wix.com/) are other alternatives that can be used. They are referred to as WYSIWYGs (what you see is what you get) platforms.

If you are semi-comfortable with your ability to set up a website, you might consider using CoffeeCup (https://www.coffeecup.com/) products if you are not ready to hand code your site or use a more in-depth program such as Adobe Dreamweaver or Muse. Once you decide which platform to use, besides GoDaddy, another inexpensive place to get hosting for your website is HostGator (https://www.hostgator.com/).

10.2 BEING PROFESSIONAL ONLINE

Whether you decide to stick with social media or to add a website, you still need to be professional online. Here are some basics for communicating effectively with other people. Some people refer to these types of guidelines as netiquette. Remember, if an activity is not acceptable face-to-face, you should not do it online either.

- Always deal with people better than you want to be treated. The online world is a dangerous place full of malicious people. You are

> ## BOX 10.1 How do you protect yourself on social media?
>
> **Greg Hardin**—*I was a heavy social media user before. In the last four or five years, I have tapered off. I've seen a lot of other people's use taper off too. It seemed to have coincided with a lot of the Snowden and NSA (National Security Agency) reports in that era. Those things seemed to have taken a lot of the innocence away from social media. It made me think twice about oversharing and what I had out there.*
>
> **kYmberly Keeton**—*Always provide a disclaimer on your "About" page. Block and delete folk on a quarterly basis that you feel are negative or do not bring out the best in you when you engage with them on social media.*
>
> **Ayla Stein**—*I have online notifications. When, somebody adds me to a list, I can see it. If the time comes, I will block a person and report them for posting threatening content.*

developing your brand, and you don't want to be perceived as someone that is a bully. For every bully, there is someone that is better at the game. Keep your conversations cordial (Box 10.1).

- Don't waste people's time with nonsense. We see it all the time with clickbait. Imagine that there is a link for an article that is supposed to be about new laws impacting libraries. But, when you click on the link, it has a video of a singing dog. The author might get the traffic, but people will not respect their content.
- Don't have false courage. Social media seems to make people think that they can say anything that they like. Sometimes social media feels downright impersonal. People online don't have to agree with what you have said. If you can't engage in meaningful discourse with them, avoid having a conversation.
- Remember that you should not write in all caps. It is the equivalent of yelling online. In addition, don't write in texting language or use a lot of emojis. You are perfecting your personal brand. What you write matters (Box 10.2).
- Write your content and give credit where it is due. If you need to use ideas from other people, include in-text citations.
- Finally, professionalism is the key. You don't need people at the office to see you with your bikini on when you are trying to be taken seriously. Consider how people might perceive your messages and pictures before you post them.

> **BOX 10.2 How do you avoid conflict on social media?**
>
> *Greg Hardin—It has helped me professionally with writing articles, presentations, and social media content. The class makes me think of telling the facts in a short and not very flowery way. I think of writing in an exact and factual style. Then if there is a sense of humor or personal aspects present, make sure it's saying what you want to say and and that there's not wiggle room for interpretation. But sometimes that irony of leaving it open to interpretation can be interesting too.*
>
> *Ayla Stein—Professionally, I just mute accounts. I use Twitter's new muting capabilities, where you can either mute a conversation or specific people. I like, where you can Tweet and then you just reply to the Tweet and it makes it one story. For me, I can think about something and then expand on it in the response Tweet. I respond to people directly. Sometimes I'll Tweet something and then think, "You know what? I don't think that came out the way that it should come out." So, I'll delete it and then try to rephrase it. I try not to do that, because, the Internet never forgets. Somebody, somewhere, has some sort of copy of it.*

10.3 ABOUT THE SOCIAL MEDIA EXPERTS

I reached out to librarians to help me to complete a study for this book. As a result, I met some amazing people while I was writing. I refer to them as social media experts. Their advice is dispersed throughout the book in textboxes. Their opinions have enriched the text. Each expert has a different librarianship focus and is at a different stage in their career and social media use. These experts are listed below.

Dr. Jason Alson is an Assistant Teaching Professor at the University of Missouri, School of Information Science and Learning Technologies. He is @SoulCitySigma on Twitter and other social media networks. His volunteer activities include being the Editor of the news magazine for the Black Caucus of the American Library Association. He researches diversity in librarianship, intellectual freedom, and information dissemination through mass media.

Greg Hardin is an Information Literacy Coordinator at the University of North Texas Libraries. His research interests include information literacy, inquiry, instruction, user experience, and technology. He is a frequent volunteer for professional organization communities and frequently speaks at conferences. He can be found on social media as @ghardin.

Kelly M. Hoppe is the Head of Research and Instructional Services at the Cornette Library at West Texas A&M University. She is a former school librarian. Her interests include digital literacy, collection development, and English language learners. She is @thebookinator on Twitter.

kYmberly Keeton is an independent publisher and art librarian. She has experience as an academic librarian, assistant professor, and as an art library coordinator. Her research interests include genealogy, digital repositories, literature, and art history. She is @kymizsofly on Twitter.

Dr. Spencer Keralis is a Research Associate Professor and Head for Digital Humanities and Collaborative Programs at the University of North Texas Libraries. He is also the Founding Director of the Digital Frontiers conference, which focuses on digital resources for humanities research, teaching, and learning. His research interests include representations of children and animals in antebellum American literature and material culture, the implications of social media, digital curation, and data management for the future of the humanities. He is a frequent speaker at conferences. He is @hauntologist on Twitter.

Ayla Stein is an Assistant Professor and Metadata Librarian at the University of Illinois of Urbana-Champaign. Her research interests include metadata, digital repositories, linked data, critical studies in LIS and technology, data curation, research data management, digital preservation, scholarly communication, digital scholarship, and intellectual property. She is a frequent speaker at conferences. She is @TheStacksCat on Twitter.

10.4 CONCLUSION

In conclusion, part of establishing your personal brand is understanding your talents and what you would like to do with your life. While you may have received training for multiple skills, personal branding should be about sharing the skills that you enjoy working with. If you can identify the skills that you are happy sharing, then your personal brand will clearly manifest itself because you are promoting something that you genuinely care about.

Authenticity in your professional life shines through and will sustain you when you feel you are not achieving your goals. You must know that the purpose that you have chosen is meaningful. Hence, it is critical to ensure that the way you brand yourself coincides with how people identify you as an expert. When you establish your purpose, think about your hobbies, volunteer experiences, and professional passion. Then you can begin to find ways to distribute your knowledge, connect with like-minded people, and acquire knowledge on social media. Eventually, your professional passion, social media branding and training, and everyday professional life should meet at a happy medium. Indeed, there is plenty to learn, many people who want to teach, and a platform for you to reach the world on social media. Best wishes to you!

APPENDIX 1

Sources for Data and Statistics

Fake news has been the focus of many local, state, national, and international discussions. One thing that combats fake news and misinformation is being aware of the facts that come from credible sources. As a thought leader, you can produce informative infographics and share information about timely topics that include facts. Moreover, correctly presenting information supported by facts can make it hard to argue with what you have written or to be misunderstood about the intent of your posts. Several websites and databases offer access to facts and statistics. The information on these websites is great for enhancing presentations, articles, and infographics.

1. United States Census Bureau: https://www.census.gov—This website hosts data collected by the United States Census Bureau about the population of the United States. Maps, graphs, tables, and downloadable data are available. The website also includes infographics and data visualizations.

2. Statista: https://www.statista.com—This website features market research about business intelligence information. Numerous tables and infographics are available, while over 60,000 topics from thousands of sources are covered.

3. The American Library Association: http://www.ala.org/tools/research/—This website provides statistics related to ALA initiatives, librarianship, the status of librarians, and library staff in the United States.

4. Stat Planet: http://www.sacmeq.org/interactive-maps/statplanet/—This website offers a browser-based data visualization tool to analyze statistics about world development.

5. Gapminder: http://www.gapminder.org/—This website provides global statistics and visualization tools to use them.

6. Fact Monster: www.factmonster.com—While this website is geared toward children, it includes works such as the Columbia Encyclopedia and Country Profiles.

7. World Statistics: http://world-statistics.org/—This website provides international statistics for countries. The data includes, but is not

limited to facts about economics, crime, tourism, public policy, and poverty.

8. United States National Center for Education Statistics (NCES): https://nces.ed.gov/—The National Center for Education Statistics is a part of the United States Department of Education that collects and shares reports based on data. Downloadable datasets are also available from this website.

9. Global Health Observatory: http://www.who.int/gho/en/—This is the World Health Organization's database of health-related statistics. Data is provided from over 150 countries with 1000 indicators that can be browsed in tables. Data can be downloaded in a variety of formats.

10. United States Data.Gov: https://www.data.gov/—This website provides public access to a repository of datasets disseminated by the Executive Branch of the United States federal government. Downloadable datasets can be browsed by topic or can be searched.

11. United States Bureau of Justice: https://www.bjs.gov/—This website compiled by the United States Bureau of Justice Statistics releases statistics about crimes, victims, the justice system, and law enforcement.

12. United States HealthData.Gov: https://www.healthdata.gov/—This is an initiative from the US Department of Health & Human Services that releases health data for use by entrepreneurs, researchers, and policymakers in hopes of stimulating analysis to improve health outcomes. Downloadable datasets are categorized and searchable.

13. US Environmental Protection Agency (EPA): https://www.epa.gov/open/data-inventory-and-activities—This is a website that includes a compilation of the data available from the EPA.

14. UNICEF: https://www.unicef.org/reports—UNICEF advocates for the rights of children in 190 countries and territories. The reports compiled to support this mission are made public on this website.

15. United States Bureau of Transportation (BTS): https://www.bts.gov/—This website provides access to surveys, reports, and data collections created by the BTS. Topics can be explored by indicators such as location and modes of transportation.

16. Geoba.se: http://www.geoba.se/—This website provides geographic information from around the world. Public domain data sources have been compiled and made searchable on this website.

17. United States Bureau of Labor Statistics: https://www.bls.gov/—This website is hosted by the United States Department of Labor. It includes datasets and tables. The data reflected examines the labor market activity, working conditions, and changes in the economy.

18. Google Public Data: https://www.google.com/publicdata/ directory—This is a public data website that helps users to explore and visualize data. It includes charts and maps. Data is provided by international organizations and academic institutions from around the world.

19. Eurostat: http://ec.europa.eu/eurostat—This is the website for the statistical office of the European Union. It provides statistics about European countries. Datasets can be downloaded in bulk and downloaded by theme.

20. Data.Gov.Uk: https://data.gov.uk/—On this website, data published by government departments and agencies in the United Kingdom. Data may be searched or browsed by themes.

21. The World Bank: https://data.worldbank.org/—The World Bank provides financial and technical assistance to developing countries. This website offers access to its global dataset.

22. DBpedia: http://wiki.dbpedia.org—This website includes a dataset created from Wikipedia articles. It allows users to query the structured information embedded within articles to conduct research.

23. The World Factbook: https://www.cia.gov/library/publications/the-world-factbook/—This is a site developed by the United States Central Intelligence Agency to provide data about 267 entities around the world. Information includes historical facts about the economy, people, government, communication, military, transportation, and international issues.

24. Pew Research Center: http://www.pewinternet.org/datasets/—Provides raw data from the Pew Research Center's research projects. The center conducts public option polls, collects demographic data, analyzes media content about attitudes and trends reflecting current events. Data is available in zip files. A registration form must be completed to use the website.

25. Information Please: https://www.infoplease.com/world/world-statistics-resources—Information Please is a website maintained by editors that provide factual information about topics related to events, culture, science, government, and history.

26. Knoema: https://www.infoplease.com/world/world-statistics-resources—As an open data resource, this website is for users that need data for reports and research. Thousands of sources have been compiled from around the world.

27. Open Data Network: https://www.opendatanetwork.com/—This is a website for sharing and finding data. Write a search term in the textbox to find datasets.

28. The European Union Open Data Portal: http://data.europa.eu/euodp/en/home—This website presents data from European Union institutions and bodies that can be used for free, both for commercial and noncommercial activities.

29. The Government of Canada Data: http://open.canada.ca/en—This a resource that offers datasets provided by the Canadian government. It includes geospatial data and apps created by the Canadian public and government.

30. Open Government Data Working Group: https://opengovernment-data.org/data/—This website is dedicated to bringing together open data published by government entities from different countries.

31. UK National Health Service (NHS) Digital: https://digital.nhs.uk/—The UK National Health Service uses this website to positively impact health care by sharing data with patients, clinicians, and researchers.

32. Amazon Web Services (AWS) Public Data Sets: https://aws.amazon.com/datasets/—Amazon describes this website as a large centralized repository of public datasets hosted at no charge.

33. George W. Bush Institute State of Our Cities: (http://www.bushcenter.org/stateofourcities/)—This resource offers education data compiled about cities in the United States. Researchers can use the data to make their own comparative analyses.

APPENDIX 2

Websites With Pictures

Pictures enhance print and online projects. This appendix is designed to provide a list of websites where photos can be found for projects. This is my disclaimer. I have not contributed pictures to these websites. In addition, I do not claim to know if all the pictures are suitable. You will have to do your own homework before using the pictures that are available. Some of these websites have ads and they require some patience to browse. Some of the pictures will have different licenses attached. Review the licenses and terms of use for each page to come to an educated decision about the content.

- #1 Free ClipArt: http://www.1clipart.com/
- Burst: https://burst.shopify.com/
- ClipArt Etc.: http://etc.usf.edu/clipart/
- Clker: www.clker.com
- Discovery Education Clipart Gallery: http://school.discoveryeducation.com/clipart/
- Iband: http://iband.com/
- Freerange: https://freerangestock.com
- FreeStockPhotography: http://www.adigitaldreamer.com/gallery/index.php
- Gratisography: https://gratisography.com/
- Hassle Free Clipart: http://www.hasslefreeclipart.com
- IM Free: http://imcreator.com/free
- MyCuteGraphics: https://www.mycutegraphics.com
- OpenClipArt: https://openclipart.org
- Pexels: https://www.pexels.com/
- Picjumbo: https://picjumbo.com/category/business/
- Pics4Learning: http://www.pics4learning.com/
- Pixabay: https://pixabay.com/
- PublicDomainVectors.org: https://publicdomainvectors.org/
- Sweet Clip Art: http://sweetclipart.com/
- Unsplash: https://unsplash.com/

United States Library Associations on Social Media

Library and Information Science (LIS) associations are at the forefront of offering training opportunities for LIS professionals. These organizations often share information that is free for both members and nonmembers. They produce newsletters that can be used to understand current trends. In addition, many of the leaders in national organizations are serving in leadership roles on the state level as well. This list of professional organizations in the United States includes the homepage, Twitter handle, Facebook, and LinkedIn page for each organization if they are available. Use these details to connect to the organization. Knowing about what is happening on the state level is just as important as understanding national issues.

Name	Home page	Twitter handle	Facebook	LinkedIn
Alabama Library Association	http://www.allanet.org/	@ALLACOM	https://www.facebook.com/AlabamaLibraryAssociation/	n/a
Alaska Library Association	http://www.akla.org/	@AKLibraryAssoc	https://www.facebook.com/AlaskaLibraryAssociation/	https://www.linkedin.com/company-beta/15576300/
Arizona Library Association	http://www.azla.org/	@azlalib	https://www.facebook.com/arizonalibraryassociation/	https://www.linkedin.com/groups/4716248/profile
California Library Association	http://www.cla-net.org/	@CaLibAssoc	https://www.facebook.com/CaliforniaLibraryAssociation/	https://www.linkedin.com/company-beta/7081798/
Colorado Association of Libraries	http://www.cal-webs.org/	@ColoAssocLibs	https://www.facebook.com/ColoradoAssociationofLibraries/	https://www.linkedin.com/groups/125900/profile
Connecticut Library Association	http://ctlibraryassociation.org/index.php	@CTLibAssoc	https://www.facebook.com/ctlibraryassociation/	https://www.linkedin.com/groups/7452386/profile
Delaware Library Association	http://dla.lib.de.us/	@DeLibAssoc	https://www.facebook.com/DelawareLibraryAssociation/	https://www.linkedin.com/company/5932248/
Florida Library Association	http://www.flalib.org/	@TweetFLAlibrary	https://www.facebook.com/FloridaLibraryAssociation/	https://www.linkedin.com/company-beta/15996136/
Georgia Library Association	http://gla.georgialibraries.org/	@GLALibrary	https://www.facebook.com/georgialibraryassociation/	https://www.linkedin.com/company-beta/15334961/
Hawai'i Library Association	http://hawaiilibrary-association.weebly.com/	@HLABoard	https://www.facebook.com/HawaiiLibraryAssociation/	n/a
Idaho Library Association	http://www.idaholibraries.org/	@IdahoLibraries	https://www.facebook.com/IdahoLibraries/	n/a
Illinois Library Association	https://www.ila.org/	@IllLibrary Assoc	https://www.facebook.com/ILibraryAssoc/	https://www.linkedin.com/company-beta/496045/
Indiana Library Federation	http://www.ilfonline.org/	@ilfonline	https://www.facebook.com/ilfonline/	https://www.linkedin.com/company-beta/1535114/
Iowa Library Association	https://www.iowalibraryassociation.org/	@IowaLA	https://www.facebook.com/IowaLibAssoc/?ref = br_rs	https://www.linkedin.com/company-beta/295233/

Name	Home page	Twitter handle	Facebook	LinkedIn
Kansas Library Association	http://kslibassoc.org/home/	n/a	https://www.facebook.com/kansaslibraryassociation/	https://www.linkedin.com/groups/2777982/profile
Kentucky Library Association	http://www.klaonline.org/	@KYLibAsn	https://www.facebook.com/KentuckyLibraryAssociation/	https://www.linkedin.com/company-beta/15323279/
Louisiana Library Association	https://llaonline.org/	n/a	https://www.facebook.com/LouisianaLibraryAssociation/	n/a
Maine Library Association	https://mainelibraries.org/	@MaineLibAssoc	https://www.facebook.com/MaineLibraryAssociation/	https://www.linkedin.com/company-beta/15960254/
Maryland Library Association	http://www.mdlib.org/	@MDLibraryAssoc	https://www.facebook.com/MDLib/	https://www.linkedin.com/company-beta/15695847/
Massachusetts Library Association	http://www.masslib.org/	@MassLibAssoc	https://www.facebook.com/Masslib	https://www.linkedin.com/company-beta/17886294/
Michigan Library Association	http://www.milibraries.org/	@MLAoffice	https://www.facebook.com/MichiganLibraryAssociation/	https://www.linkedin.com/company-beta/10593783/
Minnesota Library Association	http://www.mnlibraryassociation.org/	@MNlibraries	https://www.facebook.com/MinnesotaLibraryAssociation/	https://www.linkedin.com/company-beta/1061261/
Mississippi Library Association	http://www.mislib.org/	@MSLibraryAssoc	https://www.facebook.com/MSLibraryAssociation/	https://www.linkedin.com/company-beta/15396351/
Missouri Library Association	http://molib.org/	@MOlibraries	https://www.facebook.com/pages/Missouri-Library-Association/13274283343685	https://www.linkedin.com/company-beta/4364698/
Montana Library Association	https://mtlib.org/	@MT_mla	https://www.facebook.com/groups/34421901898/	https://www.linkedin.com/company-beta/4554841/
Nebraska Library Association	http://www.nebraskalibraries.org/	@NebLibraries	https://www.facebook.com/NebLibraries/	https://www.linkedin.com/company-beta/4476645/
Nevada Library Association	https://nevadalibraries.org/	@nvlibraries	https://www.facebook.com/nevadalibraryassociation/	https://www.linkedin.com/company-beta/15371227/
New Hampshire Library Association	http://nhlibrarians.org/	@nhlibrarians	https://www.facebook.com/groups/43106221349/	https://www.linkedin.com/company-beta/15949347/

Name	Home page	Twitter handle	Facebook	LinkedIn
New Jersey Library Association	https://www.njla.org/	@njla	https://www.facebook.com/njlibraryassociation/	https://www.linkedin.com/company-beta/4834971/
New Mexico Library Association	http://nmla.org/	@NMLib_Assn	https://www.facebook.com/NMLibraryAssociation/	n/a
New York Library Association	https://www.nyla.org/max/index.html	@NYLA_1890	https://www.facebook.com/NYLA1890/	https://www.linkedin.com/company-beta/1631228/
North Carolina Library Association	http://www.nclaonline.org/	@nclaonline	https://www.facebook.com/nclibraryassociation/	https://www.linkedin.com/groups/2720536/profile
North Dakota Library Association	http://ndla.info/index.php?bypassCookie = 1	n/a	https://www.facebook.com/North-Dakota-Library-Association-35019630345/	https://www.linkedin.com/company-beta/16045881/
Ohio Library Council	http://olc.org/	@OhioLibraryCncl	https://www.facebook.com/OhioLibraryCouncil/	https://www.linkedin.com/company-beta/15715221/
Oklahoma Library Association	http://www.oklibs.org/	@oklibs	https://www.facebook.com/oklibs/	https://www.linkedin.com/company-beta/4486760/
Oregon Library Association	http://www.olaweb.org/	@OregonLibraries	https://www.facebook.com/OregonLibraries/	https://www.linkedin.com/groups/12043283/profile
Pennsylvania Library Association	http://www.palibraries.org/	@PALibraryAssoc	https://www.facebook.com/PALibraries/	https://www.linkedin.com/groups/2029279/profile
Rhode Island Library Association	http://www.rilibraries.org/	@rilalibs	https://www.facebook.com/rilibraries/	https://www.linkedin.com/company-beta/15690467/
South Carolina Library Association	http://www.scla.org/	@sclanews	https://www.facebook.com/southcarolinalibraryassociation/	https://www.linkedin.com/company-beta/16048768/
South Dakota Library Association	http://www.sdlibraryassociation.org/	n/a	https://www.facebook.com/SouthDakotaLibraryAssociation/	https://www.linkedin.com/company-beta/15509168/
Tennessee Library Association	http://www.tnla.org/	@TNLA	https://www.facebook.com/TennesseeLibraryAssociation/	https://www.linkedin.com/company-beta/15347100/
Texas Library Association	http://www.txla.org/	@TXLA	https://www.facebook.com/TexasLibraryAssociation/	https://www.linkedin.com/company-beta/301473/

Name	Home page	Twitter handle	Facebook	LinkedIn
Utah Library Association	http://ula.org/	@UtahLibAssoc	https://www.facebook.com/ UtahLibraryAssociation/	https://www.linkedin.com/ company-beta/15583544/
Vermont Library Association	http://www. vermontlibraries.org/	@VLAlib	https://www.facebook.com/ VTLibraryAssociation/	https://www.linkedin.com/ company-beta/16057694/
Virginia Library Association	http://www.vla.org/	@VirginiaLibrary	https://www.facebook.com/ VALibraryAssociation/	https://www.linkedin.com/ company-beta/3984522/
Washington Library Association	http://www.wla.org/	@WALIBASSN	https://www.facebook.com/ WashingtonLibraryAssociation/	https://www.linkedin.com/ company-beta/522581/
District of Columbia Library Association	https://www.dcla.org/	@DCLALibrarians	https://www.facebook.com/groups/ 24861967157/	https://www.linkedin.com/ groups/4399105/profile
West Virginia Library Association	http://wvla.org/index. php	@WestVirginiaLib	https://www.facebook.com/ WestVirginiaLibraries/	n/a
Wisconsin Library Association	http://wla. wisconsinlibraries.org/	@WisconsinLibs	https://www.facebook.com/ WisconsinLibraries/	https://www.linkedin.com/ company-beta/15707395/
Wyoming Library Association	http://www.wyla.org/	n/a	https://www.facebook.com/ WyoLibraryAssociation/	https://www.linkedin.com/ company-beta/15647524/

APPENDIX 4

Social Media Networks and Tools

This book focuses on social media tools that librarians can use for professional development and personal branding. While the most popular tools have been discussed, there are hundreds more to explore. This list provides a starting point so that readers can begin to develop social media content and participate in activities. The list has several categories that include blogging, digital curation, creating wikis, collaborating, crowdsourcing content, digital storytelling, scheduling events, live streaming and posting videos, online discussions, podcasting, social networks for researchers, and microblogging. Explore the list to find tools that can make you more productive with social media. There are tools suitable for technology beginners and experts.

Social media tools and networks

Name	Purpose	Link
Storify	Blogging	https://storify.com/
Blogs.com	Blogging	http://www.typepad.com/
Xanga	Blogging	http://xanga.com/
Reddit	Blogging	https://www.reddit.com/
Wordpress	Blogging	https://wordpress.com
Blogger	Blogging	https://www.blogger.com/about/?r = 2
TypePad	Blogging	http://www.typepad.com/
WordPress.Org	Blogging	https://wordpress.org
WordPress.com	Blogging	https://wordpress.com/
Edublogs	Blogging	https://edublogs.org/
Squarespace	Blogging and website creating	https://www.squarespace.com
Google +	Collaborating	https://plus.google.com/discover
Zoho	Collaborating	https://www.zoho.com/
Slack	Collaborating	https://slack.com/
Asana	Collaborating	https://asana.com/
Ryver	Collaborating	https://ryver.com/

(Continued)

Social media tools and networks

Name	Purpose	Link
Trello	Collaborating	https://trello.com/
Google +	Collaborating	https://plus.google.com/ discover
Zoho	Collaborating	https://www.zoho.com/
Slack	Collaborating	https://slack.com/
Asana	Collaborating	https://asana.com/
Ryver	Collaborating	https://ryver.com/
Trello	Collaborating	https://trello.com/
Google Docs	Create and edit documents online	https://www.google.com/
Twiki	Creating Wikis	http://twiki.org/
Zoho Wiki	Creating Wikis	https://www.zoho.com/ wiki/
Xwiki	Creating Wikis	http://www.xwiki.org/ xwiki/bin/view/Main/ WebHome
DokuWiki	Creating Wikis	https://www.dokuwiki.org/ dokuwiki#
PBWorks	Creating Wikis	http://www.pbworks.com/
Wikipedia	Crowdsourcing content	https://www.wikipedia.org/
Reddit	Crowdsourcing content	https://www.reddit.com/
Buzzfeed	Crowdsourcing content	https://www.buzzfeed.com/
Pearltrees	Digital curation	https://www.pearltrees.com/
Paper.li	Digital curation	https://paper.li/
Scoop.it	Digital curation	https://www.scoop.it/
Diigo	Digital curation	https://www.diigo.com/
Delicious	Digital curation	https://del.icio.us/
eLink	Digital curation	https://elink.io
Pinterest	Digital curation	https://www.pinterest.com/
Padlet	Digital curation	https://www.padlet.com
Screencast-O-Matic	Digital storytelling	https://screencast-o-matic. com/
Biteable	Digital storytelling	https://biteable.com/
Adobe Spark	Digital storytelling	https://spark.adobe.com/ about/page
Office Sway	Digital storytelling	https://sway.com/
Storybird	Digital storytelling	https://storybird.com/
PowToon	Digital storytelling	http://www.powtoon.com/
NearPod	Digital storytelling and presentations	https://nearpod.com/
Go To Meeting	Hosting events	https://gotomeeting.com

(*Continued*)

Social media tools and networks

Name	Purpose	Link
Livestream	Live streaming and posting videos	https://livestream.com/
Ustream	Live streaming and posting videos	http://www.ustream.tv/
Airtime	Live streaming and posting videos	https://www.airtime.com/
Flixwagon	Live streaming and posting videos	https://www.flixwagon.com/
YouTube	Live streaming and posting videos	https://www.youtube.com
Disqus	Making comments	https://disqus.com
Intensedebate	Making comments	https://www.intensedebate.com/
Yelp	Making comments	https//www.yelp.com
Tumblr	Microblogging and social networking	https://www.tumblr.com/
Twitter	Microcommunications and microblogging	https://twitter.com/?
Utterz	Microcommunications and microblogging	http://utterz.com/
Flipgrid	Online video discussions	https://info.flipgrid.com/
Spreaker	Podcasting	https://www.spreaker.com/
Vimeo	Posting videos	https://www.vimeo.com
Feedly	RSS feeds	https://feedly.com/i/welcome
Eventbrite	Schedule events	https://www.eventbrite.com/
Upcoming	Schedule events	https://upcoming.org
Meetup	Schedule events	https://www.meetup.com/
YouTube	Sharing and watching videos	youtube.com
Box	Sharing documents and content	https://www.box.com/
Dropbox	Sharing documents and content	https://www.dropbox.com/
Flickr	Sharing pictures	https://www.flickr.com/
Multiply	Sharing pictures	http://www.multiply.com/
SmugMug	Sharing pictures	https://www.smugmug.com/
Photobucket	Sharing pictures	http://photobucket.com/

(*Continued*)

Social media tools and networks

Name	Purpose	Link
Shutterfly	Sharing pictures	https://www.shutterfly.com/
Hipstamatic	Sharing pictures	http://hipstamatic.com/camera/
Instagram	Sharing pictures and videos	https://www.instagram.com/?hl = en
Tumbler	Sharing pictures and videos	https://www.tumblr.com/
SnapChat	Sharing pictures and videos	https://www.snapchat.com/
Prezi	Sharing presentations	https://prezi.com/
Slideshare	Sharing presentations	https://www.slideshare.net/
Speaker Deck	Sharing presentations	https://speakerdeck.com
Knovio	Sharing presentations	https://www.knovio.com
Freshdesk	Sharing videos	https://freshdesk.com/
Vimeo	Sharing videos	https://vimeo.com/
Facebook	Sharing with family, friends, and acquaintances	https://www.facebook.com/
MySpace	Sharing with family, friends, and acquaintances	https://myspace.com/
Diigo	Social bookmarking	https://www.diigo.com/
Evernote	Social bookmarking	https://evernote.com/
Del.icio.us	Social bookmarking	https://del.icio.us/
StumbleUpon	Social bookmarking	https://www.stumbleupon.com/
Pocket	Social bookmarking	https://getpocket.com/
Instapaper	Social bookmarking	https://www.instapaper.com/
HootSuite	Social media dashboard	https://www.hootsuite.com
NetVibes	Social media dashboard	https://www.netvibes.com
Academia.Edu	Social network for researchers	https://www.academia.edu/
ResearchGate	Social network for researchers	https://www.researchgate.net/
Google Scholar	Social network for researchers	https://scholar.google.com/
Facebook	Social network	https://www.facebook.com/
Tagged	Social network	https://secure.tagged.com/
Google +	Social network	https://plus.google.com/
Bebo	Social network	https://bebo.com/

(Continued)

Social media tools and networks

Name	Purpose	Link
Hi5	Social network	https://secure.hi5.com/?
Soci	Social network	https://www.meetsoci.com/
Twitter	Social network	https://twitter.com/
Empire Avenue	Social network	https://play.empire.kred/
Myspace	Social network	https://myspace.com/
Tweetbot	Twitter support	https://tapbots.com/ tweetbot/
TweetCaster	Twitter support	http://tweetcaster.com/
TweetDeck	Twitter support	https://tweetdeck.twitter. com/
Twitterfall	Twitter support	https://twitterfall.com/

APPENDIX 5

Online Professional Development Sources for Librarians

Professional development is a necessary component of growing a career that can be costly. Not only is professional development costly but also time-consuming. Many times, it does not fit into work schedules. Finding professional development activities to complete in the comfort of the home is an excellent approach to learning about the trends and guidelines that are impacting library and information science (LIS). This list offers the website, blog, Facebook, and Twitter links to various organizations offering professional development pertinent to LIS professionals. Announcements and handouts for professional development are often placed on social media to serve as alerts to those interested in participating or receiving information.

Online professional development sources for librarians

Organization name	Official website	Blog	Facebook	Twitter
Accessible Technology Coalition	https://atcoalition.org/training/	https://atcoalition.org/atc-blog/	https://www.facebook.com/ATCoalition/	
Association of College & Research Libraries eLearning	http://www.ala.org/acrl/onlinelearning/	http://acrlog.org/	https://www.facebook.com/ala.acrl/	https://twitter.com/ALA_ACRL
Adlit: All About Adolescent Literacy	http://www.adlit.org/	http://www.adlit.org/adlit_blogs/	https://www.facebook.com/AdLit.org/	https://twitter.com/adlit
AERA: American Educational Research Association	http://www.aera.net/	http://www.aera.net/About-AERA/Member-Constituents/Divisions/	https://www.facebook.com/AERAEdResearch	https://twitter.com/AERA_EdResearch
American Library Association	http://www.ala.org/onlinelearning/	http://www.ala.org/blog	https://www.facebook.com/AmericanLibraryAssociation/	https://twitter.com/ALALibrary
American Libraries Magazine	https://americanlibrariesmagazine.org/tag/dewey-decibel/	https://americanlibrariesmagazine.org/blogs/	https://www.facebook.com/amlibraries/	https://twitter.com/amlibraries
Arizona State Library, Archives & Public Records	https://www.azlibrary.gov/libdev		https://www.facebook.com/pages/Arizona-State-Library-Archives-and-Public-Records-Building/190039388055170	https://twitter.com/StateLibAZ
Association for Information Science and Technology	https://www.asist.org/	https://www.asist.org/blog/		https://twitter.com/asist_org?lang=en

Online professional development sources for librarians

Organization name	Official website	Blog	Facebook	Twitter
Association of College & Research Libraries	http://www.ala.org/acrl	http://www.ala.org/acrl/cjcls-blog	https://www.facebook.com/ala.acrl/	https://twitter.com/ALA_ACRL
Association for Library Collections & Technical Services	http://www.ala.org/alcts/	http://www.ala.org/alctsnews/	https://www.facebook.com/ALCTS/	https://twitter.com/ALCTS_CE
Association of Research Libraries	http://www.arl.org	http://www.arl.org/news/blog	https://www.facebook.com/association.of.research.libraries	https://twitter.com/ARLnews
ASCD Professional Learning	http://www.ascd.org/professional-development.aspx	http://inservice.ascd.org/	https://www.facebook.com/ascd.org	https://twitter.com/ASCD
Blended Librarians Online Learning Community	http://blendedlibrarian.learningtimes.net/	http://blendedlibrarian.learningtimes.net/blblog/#.WRsJJWjyuUk	https://www.facebook.com/BlendedLibrarians/	https://twitter.com/blendedlib
Chronicle of Higher Education	http://www.chronicle.com/	http://www.chronicle.com/section/Blogs/164/?cid = UCHESIDENAV1	https://www.facebook.com/chronicle.of.higher.education	https://twitter.com/chronicle
Chartered Institute of Library and Information Professionals (CILIP)	https://www.cilip.org.uk/	https://www.cilip.org.uk/blog	https://www.facebook.com/CILIPinfo/	https://twitter.com/CILIPinfo
Common Sense Education	https://www.commonsensemedia.org/educators	https://www.commonsense.org/education/blog	https://www.facebook.com/CommonSenseEd	https://twitter.com/CommonSenseEd
Coursera	https://www.coursera.org/	https://blog.coursera.org/	https://www.facebook.com/Coursera	https://twitter.com/coursera
EDUCAUSE Learning Initiative	https://www.educause.edu/eli	http://er.educause.edu/blogs	https://www.facebook.com/EDUCAUSE	https://twitter.com/educause

Online professional development sources for librarians

Organization name	Official website	Blog	Facebook	Twitter
edWeb	http://home.edweb.net/	http://home.edweb.net/category/blog/		https://twitter.com/edwebnet
Faculty Focus	https://www.facultyfocus.com/	https://www.facultyfocus.com/topic/articles/teaching-professor-blog/	https://www.facebook.com/facultyfocus	https://twitter.com/facultyfocus
Google for Education	https://edu.google.com/higher-education/	https://blog.google/topics/education/	https://plus.google.com/+GoogleforEducation	https://twitter.com/googleforedu
Hack Library School	https://hacklibraryschool.com/		https://www.facebook.com/hacklibschool	https://twitter.com/hacklibschool?lang = en
International Federation of Library Associations (IFLA)	https://www.ifla.org/	https://blogs.ifla.org/arl/	https://www.facebook.com/IFLA.org/	https://twitter.com/IFLA
Inside Higher Ed	https://www.insidehighered.com/	https://www.insidehighered.com/blogs/	https://www.facebook.com/InsideHigherEdDC/	https://twitter.com/insidehighered
Institute of Museum and Library Services (IMLS)	https://www.imls.gov/	https://www.imls.gov/news-events/upnext-blog/	https://www.facebook.com/USIMLS	https://twitter.com/us_imls
International Society for Technology in Education (ISTE)	http://www.iste.org/	http://librariansnetwork.weebly.com/	https://www.facebook.com/groups/istesiglib/	https://twitter.com/istelib
Library 2.0	http://www.library20.com/	http://www.library20.com/profiles/blog/list		https://twitter.com/hashtag/library20
Library Journal	https://lj.libraryjournal.com/		https://www.facebook.com/pg/libraryjournalmagazine/posts/	https://twitter.com/LibraryJournal
Library Juice Academy	http://libraryjuiceacademy.com/index.php	http://libraryjuiceacademy.com/news/	https://www.facebook.com/LibraryJuiceAcademy	https://twitter.com/LibJuiceAcademy

Online professional development sources for librarians

Organization name	Official website	Blog	Facebook	Twitter
Microsoft Education	https://www.microsoft.com/en-us/education/default.aspx	https://educationblog.microsoft.com/	https://www.facebook.com/microsoftineducation/	https://twitter.com/msphilanthropic
OCLC Research	http://www.oclc.org/research.html	http://www.oclc.org/research/publications/blogs.html.html	https://www.facebook.com/OCLCResearch/	https://twitter.com/OCLC
PBS Teacherline	http://www.pbs.org/teacherline/		https://www.facebook.com/pbsteacherline	https://twitter.com/pbsteacherline
WebJunction	http://www.webjunction.org/	http://www.webjunction.org/explore-topics/digital-inclusion/news.html/	https://www.facebook.com/WebJunctionNews	https://twitter.com/WebJunction

Blogs for Librarians

Librarians create blogs about every imaginable topic related to library and information science. Reading these blogs can serve as an informal method of professional development. Many blogs also include RSS feeds that can be subscribed to remove the need for visiting them each day. Reading these blogs can help you to determine what niche you should focus on for your personal branding. They will also indicate how other librarian and information science professionals are approaching personal branding for themselves. Use this list of librarians with blogs and blogs about librarians to get you started on your search for professional development.

Librarian blogs

Title	URL
Academic Librarian	https://blogs.princeton.edu/librarian/
Academic Writing Librarians	http://academicwritinglibrarian.blogspot.com/
ACRL Value of Academic Libraries	http://www.acrl.ala.org/value/
ACRLog	http://acrlog.org/
A Library Writer's Blog	http://librarywriting.blogspot.com/
Beyond the Job	http://www.beyondthejob.org/
Blended Librarian Blog	http://blendedlibrarian.learningtimes.net/blblog/#.WNMnrPnyuUl
Confessions of a Science Librarian	http://scienceblogs.com/confessions/
Delores' List of CFPs	http://sites.psu.edu/doloreslistofcfps/
Designer Librarian	https://designerlibrarian.wordpress.com/
Designing Better Libraries	http://dbl.lishost.org/blog/#.WNMqnvnyuUl
Every Library	http://everylibrary.org/
Free Range Librarian	http://freerangelibrarian.com/
Gypsy Librarian	http://gypsylibrarian.blogspot.com/
HNet	https://networks.h-net.org/h-announce?type = CFPs

(Continued)

Librarian blogs

Title	URL
IFLA Blogs: Academic and Research Libraries Section	https://blogs.ifla.org/arl/
iLOVE: Library Instruction for the Rest of Us	http://ilove-instruction.blogspot.com/
Info-fetishist	https://info-fetishist.org/
Information Literacy Weblog	http://information-literacy.blogspot.com/
INFORMATION Wants To Be Free	http://meredith.wolfwater.com/wordpress/
Lauren's Library Blog	http://laurenpressley.com/library/
Librarians Matter	http://www.librariansmatter.com/blog/
Libraries + Inquiry	https://veronicaarellanodouglas.com/
Library Babel Fish	https://www.insidehighered.com/blogs/library-babel-fish
Mr. Library Dude	https://mrlibrarydude.wordpress.com/
Musings about Librarianship	http://musingsaboutlibrarianship.blogspot.com/
Musings of a Lady Librarian	http://sarahvisintini.com/
Pegasus Librarian	http://pegasuslibrarian.com/
Pumped Librarian	http://pumpedlibrarian.blogspot.com/
Rule Number One: A Library Blog	https://rulenumberoneblog.com/
Scholarly Communications @ Duke	http://blogs.library.duke.edu/scholcomm/
Service Learning Librarian	https://www.libraries.wright.edu/community/servicelearning/
The Researching Librarian	http://www.researchinglibrarian.com/
Thoughts from Carl Grant	http://thoughts.care-affiliates.com/
Undergraduate Science Librarian	https://undergraduatesciencelibrarian.org/

Hashtags for Librarians

Hashtags can be thought of as keywords that are used for organizing conversations and searching on social media. Each one begins with a pound or number sign (#). Hashtags work across platforms such as Twitter and Facebook. They are a defining factor in the functionality of a Twitter Chat. This appendix contains several hashtags related to library and information science. Each hashtag has a short subject descriptor to define it. Hashtags are continuously developed each day. However, these are enough to get started with finding conversations to follow on social media.

Hashtags for librarians

Hashtags	Subject
#alscchat	Association of Library Science to Children chat focused on providing exemplary service to children
#auslibchat	Australian library chat for library students and professionals
#bookmail	Designed to share books
#bookstagram	Promotes books and reading
#code4lib	Coding in libraries
#colorourcollection	Library coloring events
#critlib	Critical librarianship
#datalibs	Data and data services in libraries
#dearHLS	Hack Library School information for prospective students
#edtechbridge	Educational technology
#edtechchat	Library chat for educational technology
#Engchat	Relationships with students through books
#flipgrid	Social learning with videos
#inaljchat	Finding library jobs
#infolit	Information about literacy and libraries
#Instructionaldesign	Teaching and learning, faculty development
#interlibnet	Librarian mentoring and developing international relationship
#libchat	Chat for libraries, books, and technology
#libleadgender	Gender issues related to library leadership

(Continued)

Hashtags for librarians

Hashtags	Subject
#librarianproblems	Related to problems with working in libraries
#librarylife	Conversations about working in libraries
#libraryproblems	Issues related to library work
#libtechwomen	Networking, skill development, and technology
#lisjob	LIS jobs
#lisprochat	Chat about trends in libraries
#pblchat	Project-based learning chat
#radlibchat	Radical librarian chat
#readingresilienceproject	Recommendations for books and topics to read about
#saturdaylibrarian	Librarians that work on the weekend
#scholcomm	Scholarly communication
#tlchat	Teacher librarian chat
#UKlibchat	UK Chat about libraries
#UXlibs	User experience in libraries

APPENDIX 8

Librarians on Twitter

Twitter has a diverse and robust community of librarians that specialize in every library and information science (LIS) subject available. Some are even creating new areas of specialties. Here is a list to get you started with searching for librarians on Twitter. Many of these librarians maintain blogs and websites that are linked from their Twitter pages. Often, their profiles describe the topics that they are passionate about. Reviewing their Tweets will also help you to identify new hashtags and subjects outside of LIS that are pertinent to the field. There are thousands of librarians participating. A longer list is maintained by Giso Borman (@giso6150) and can be found at https://twitter.com/giso6150/lists/libraryland/members.

Librarians on Twitter

Name	Home page	Handle
Donna Witek	https://twitter.com/donnarosemary	@donnarosemary
Joe Hardenbrook	https://twitter.com/mrlibrarydude	@mrlibrarydude
Violet Fox	https://twitter.com/violetfox	@violetfox
Spencer Keralis	https://twitter.com/hauntologist	@hauntologist
kYmberly Keeton	https://twitter.com/kymizsofly	@kymizsofly
Jason Alston	https://twitter.com/SoulCitySigma	@SoulCitySigma
Martin O'Connor	https://twitter.com/martinoconnor3	@martinoconnor3
Krista Godfrey	https://twitter.com/weelibrarian	@weelibrarian
Catherine Reid	https://twitter.com/CatherineAReid	@CatherineAReid
Lauren Hays	https://twitter.com/Lib_Lauren	@Lib_Lauren
Carla James	https://twitter.com/james_carla	@james_carla
Carli Spina	https://twitter.com/CarliSpina	@CarliSpina
Diane L. Schrecker	https://twitter.com/dschrecker	@dschrecker
Jess Isler	https://twitter.com/jessisler	@ jessisler
Lisa Hubbell	https://twitter.com/lisahubbell	@lisahubbell

(Continued)

Librarians on Twitter

Name	Home page	Handle
The Info Sherpa	https://twitter.com/TheInfoSherpa	@TheInfoSherpa
Judy O'Connell	https://twitter.com/heyjudeonline	@heyjudeonline
Greg Hardin	https://twitter.com/ghardin	@ghardin
Katherine Ahnberg	https://twitter.com/teach_research	@teach_research
Michelle Rubino	https://twitter.com/OssusLibrarian	@OssusLibrarian
Sue Vasakas	https://twitter.com/SuetheLibrarian	@SuetheLibrarian
Wayne Bivens-Tatum	https://twitter.com/acadlibrarian	@acadlibrarian
Michelle Goodridge	https://twitter.com/migoodridge	@migoodridge
Jane Schmidt	https://twitter.com/janeschmidt	@janeschmidt
Krystal Appiah	https://twitter.com/kaappiah	@kaappiah
Sue House	https://twitter.com/uswsuehouse	@uswsuehouse
Steven Chang	https://twitter.com/StevenPChang	@StevenPChang
Kelly Hoppe	https://twitter.com/thebookinator	@thebookinator
Jeff Karlsen	https://twitter.com/JeffatSCC	@JeffatSCC
Stephanie Livengood	https://twitter.com/Researchtweeter	@Researchtweeter
Annie Gleeson	https://twitter.com/Annie_Bob	@Annie_Bob
Sharlene Paxton	https://twitter.com/SharlenePaxton	@SharlenePaxton
Alyssa Jocson Porter	https://twitter.com/itsuhLEEsuh	@itsuhLEEsuh
Kirstie Preest	https://twitter.com/kirstiewales	@kirstiewales
Eamon Tewell	https://twitter.com/EamonTewell	@EamonTewell
Elizabeth Hutchinson	https://twitter.com/Elizabethutch	@Elizabethutch
Graeme Oke	https://twitter.com/GraemeO28	@GraemeO28
Laura Saunders	https://twitter.com/bibliolaura	@bibliolaura
Jess Emerton	https://twitter.com/JessEmerton	@JessEmerton
Merinda Kaye Hensley	https://twitter.com/mhensle1	@mhensle1
Esther Grassian	https://twitter.com/estherg	@estherg

(*Continued*)

Librarians on Twitter

Name	Home page	Handle
C Doi	https://twitter.com/cdoi	@cdoi
Chaitra Powell	https://twitter.com/chaitrapeezy	@chaitrapeezy
Sophie Bury	https://twitter.com/sophbury	@sophbury
Nazlin Bhimani	https://twitter.com/ NazlinBhimani	@NazlinBhimani
Lorena O'English	https://twitter.com/wsulorena	@wsulorena
Amy Hildreth Chen	https://twitter.com/ AmyHildrethChen	@AmyHildrethChen
Merralin	https://twitter.com/Merralin	@Merralin
Andy Horton	https://twitter.com/fechtbuch	@fechtbuch
Zoe Fisher	https://twitter.com/zoh_zoh	@zoh_zoh
Michelle Breen	https://twitter.com/ michellebreenUL	@michellebreenUL

APPENDIX 9

Library Job Websites and Social Media Links

There are many jobs available for library and information science (LIS) professionals. Yet, it can be difficult to search through multiple websites for these jobs. Twitter and Facebook host several pages for organizations that have jobs posted relevant to LIS. This appendix includes a list of some of these organizations. The title of each organization, their website link, and their social media links are included. It is possible to subscribe too many of the websites and blogs using RSS feeds. Services like HootSuite and IFTTT can be used to curate a list or automate the search process for jobs as well.

Library job websites and social media links

Organization	Website	Social media link
Association of College & Research Libraries (ACRL) Residency Interest Group	http://acrl.ala.org/residency/	https://twitter.com/ACRL_RIG
American Library Association (ALA) Jobs	https://joblist.ala.org/	https://twitter.com/ALA_JobLIST
American Theological Library Association	https://www.atla.com/Members/development/jobs/Pages/default.aspx	https://twitter.com/YourATLA https://www.facebook.com/AmericanTheologicalLibraryAssociation
Association of Research Libraries (ARL)	http://www.arl.org/	https://twitter.com/ARLnews https://www.facebook.com/association.of.research.libraries/
Association for Information Science & Technology (ASIS&T)	https://asist-jobs.careerwebsite.com/	https://twitter.com/asist_org
Against the Grain: Job Bank	http://www.against-the-grain.com/category/jobs/	https://twitter.com/ATG_NewsChannel
American Association of Law Libraries Career Center	http://careers.aallnet.org/jobs/	https://twitter.com/aallnet
Association of Research Libraries	http://www.arl.org/leadership-recruitment/job-listings#search-form/	https://twitter.com/ARLnews
Australian Library and Information Association	https://www.alia.org.au/jobs	https://twitter.com/ALIANational https://www.facebook.com/ALIANational/
British & Irish Association of Law Librarians	https://biall.org.uk/careers/jobs/	https://twitter.com/biall_uk
British Columbia Library Association	https://partnershipjobs.ca//	https://twitter.com/bclaconnect
	https://www.cilip.org.uk/	https://twitter.com/CILIPinfo

Library job websites and social media links

Organization	Website	Social media link
Chartered Institute of Library and Information Professionals (CILIP)		https://www.facebook.com/CILIPinfo/
Consortium of Academic and Research Libraries in Illinois	https://www.carli.illinois.edu/jobs	https://twitter.com/CARLIoffice
Glen Recruitment	http://www.glenrecruitment.co.uk/	https://twitter.com/GlenRecruitment
Hiring Librarians	https://hiringlibrarians.com/	https://twitter.com/HiringLib
INALJ (I Need A Library Job)	http://inalj.com/	https://twitter.com/inaljnaomi
JINFO	https://www.jinfo.com/	https://twitter.com/JinfoResearch/
		https://www.facebook.com/Jinfo-Limited-33926274353/
LAC FEDERAL	https://lacfederal.com/	https://twitter.com/lacfederal
LIScareer.com	http://www.liscareer.com/	https://www.facebook.com/liscareer/
LibGig	https://www.libgig.com/	https://twitter.com/libgig
Libjobs	http://www.libjobs.com/	https://twitter.com/LibJobs_board
		https://www.facebook.com/libjobs4you/
Library Association of Ireland	http://www.libraryassociation.ie/career/find-and-advertise-jobs	https://twitter.com/libraryireland
		https://www.facebook.com/Library-Association-of-Ireland-10447863224/
Library and Information Technology Association	http://www.ala.org/lita/professional/jobs/looking	https://twitter.com/ala_lita?lang = en
		https://www.facebook.com/LITA.ALA/
Library Job Online	https://www.libraryjobonline.org/	https://twitter.com/libraryjobline/
Library Journal Job Zone	http://jobs.libraryjournal.com/	https://www.facebook.com/libraryjournalmagazine/
		https://twitter.com/LibraryJournal
Library of Congress Opportunities	https://www.loc.gov/careers/	https://twitter.com/librarycongress

Library job websites and social media links

Organization	Website	Social media link
Libraryjobs.ie	http://libraryjobs.ie/	https://twitter.com/libraryjobs
MLA (Medical Library Association)	http://www.mlanet.org/jobs/	https://twitter.com/MedLibAssn
		https://www.facebook.com/ MedicalLibraryAssn
NASIG Jobs	http://www.nasig.org/	https://nasigjobs.wordpress.com/
		https://twitter.com/NASIG
Pacific Northwest Library Association	http://www.pnla.org/jobs	https://twitter.com/PNLA_Org
		https://www.facebook.com/pnla.org/
Society of American Archivists	http://careers.archivists.org/jobs	https://twitter.com/archivists_org
		https://www.facebook.com/archivists
Special Libraries Association Job Listings	https://careers.sla.org	https://www.linkedin.com/company/sla
		https://www.facebook.com/slahq
		https://twitter.com/slahq
TFPL	https://www.tfpl.com/job-search/	https://twitter.com/tfpl_Ltd

APPENDIX 10

Fair Use Myths and Facts

Copyright and Fair Use are topics that can be intimidating on the surface. Copyright law is a constitutional law which automatically offers legal protection to the original work of authors. Fair use offers exceptions to copyright law under specific conditions. Fair use is defined as "a legal doctrine that promotes freedom of expression by permitting the unlicensed use of copyright-protected works in certain circumstances" (U.S. Copyright Office, 2017, p. 6). This appendix consists of an infographic created by the Association of Research Libraries (2017). The infographic discusses myths and facts about Fair Use to help scholars understand best practices.

Fair Use Myths & Facts

 Many myths persist about fair use, an essential right that allows the use of copyrighted material without permission from the copyright holder under certain circumstances. We debunk some of the most common fair use myths here.

Myth: Fair use is a defense, or minor exception, not a right.
Fact: Fair use is a right that accommodates the First Amendment.

Fair use is a right explicitly recognized by the Copyright Act.[1] The Supreme Court has recognized this right as a "First Amendment safeguard" because copyright law might otherwise constrict freedom of speech.

Myth: Copyright's primary purpose is rewarding authors and not promoting the public benefit.
Fact: The US Constitution clearly states that the purpose of the intellectual property system is to "promote the progress of science and the useful arts."

The Supreme Court has repeatedly stressed that the intellectual property system must support the Constitutional rationale and, "The immediate effect of our copyright law is to secure a fair return for an 'author's' creative labor. But the ultimate aim is, by this incentive, to stimulate artistic creativity for the general public good."[2] Fair use promotes this rationale by ensuring works can be used for a variety of purposes.

Myth: Where a specific limitation or exception exists under copyright law, fair use does not apply.
Fact: Fair use is a right that exists in addition to specific exceptions.

While specific exceptions provide certainty for particular activities or apply where fair use does not, the fair use doctrine remains an important right that is flexible and responsive to new technologies and developments, as confirmed by courts.[3]

Myth: There is no guidance on fair use.
Fact: The statute, numerous court decisions, and best practices provide ample guidance.

Section 107 of the Copyright Act lays out four factors and also includes a non exhaustive list of purposes that may be fair use. A multitude of court decisions also provide direction on fair use, particularly with respect to whether a use is transformative and therefore more likely to be considered fair use. Best practices,[4] often grounded in court decisions, similarly provide helpful guidance by summarizing the best practices of a particular community.

1. Section 108(f)(4) of the Copyright Act specifically references "the right of fair use as provided by section 107."
2. Feist Publications, Inc. v. Rural Television Services Co., 499 U.S. 340 (1991).
3. See, e.g., Authors Guild v. HathiTrust. The Second Circuit rejected the claim that Section 108 renders fair use inapplicable because of the plain language of the statute. Additionally, it found the creation of accessible format works for the print disabled was fair use and, as a result, "we need not consider" whether the activity was permissible under Section 121.
4. Codes of best practices have been created for a variety of communities and purposes. For numerous examples, see Center for Media & Social Impact, "Best Practices," accessed January 19, 2017, http://archive.cmsimpact.org/fair-use/best-practices.

Figure A10.1 (A) Fair use Myths and Facts Infographic Part 1. (B) Fair use Myths and Facts Infographic Part 2.

Figure A10.1 (Continued)

REFERENCES

Association of Research Libraries. (2017). Fair use myths and facts. Retrieved from ⟨http://fairuseweek.org/wp-content/uploads/2017/02/fair-use-myths-and-facts-info-graphic-feb2017.pdf⟩ (accessed 2018.02.21).

U.S. Copyright Office. (2017). Copyright basics. Retrieved from ⟨https://www.copy-right.gov/circs/circ01.pdf⟩ (accessed 2018.01.21).

INDEX

Printed in the United States
By Bookmasters